The 500 Hidden Secrets of
BRUSSELS

INTRODUCTION

———

This book is written for readers who want to discover the hidden side of Brussels. It lists the places the author would recommend to friends if they asked him where they should go in Brussels. It doesn't mention everything there is to see, but concentrates on the less well-known places that reflect the city's understated charm.

Here you will find the 5 best places to eat frites, the 5 small museums that no one should miss and the 5 best record shops in town.

The aim is to reveal the secret gems that most people do not know about, like the cafeteria on the top floor of the national library, or the metro station that is decorated with 140 characters from Tintin albums, or the art cinema that seats just 20 people.

This is also a guide to the people who have shaped Brussels. You will meet the painter René Magritte, who dressed each morning in a suit and tie, and then proceeded to paint some of the world's most disturbing images. You will also encounter the comic book illustrator Hergé, who created the adventures of Tintin, and the architect Victor Horta, who designed houses that were unlike anything ever built before.

This is meant to be a gentle introduction to the other side of Brussels, the Brussels that almost no one knows, not even the Belgians. You do not have to do everything in the book, but you are urged at the very least to drink a beer in one of the 5 best bars, eat at one of the 5 best fish restaurants, and visit one of the 5 best small museums.

HOW TO USE THIS BOOK?

This book contains 500 things about Brussels in 100 different categories. Some are places to visit. Others are bits of information. The aim is to inspire, not to cover the city from A to Z.

The places listed in the guide are given an address, a district and a number. The district and number allow you to find the locations on the maps at the beginning of this book.

You need to bear in mind that cities change all the time. The chef who hits a high note one day can be uninspired on the day you happen to visit. The hotel ecstatically reviewed in this book might suddenly go downhill under a new manager. The bar considered one of the 5 best in Brussels might turn out to be empty on the night you visit.

This is obviously a highly personal selection. You might not always agree with it. You are invited to send comments and updates to the author and publisher at *info@lusterweb.com*. Or leave a message on the website *www.mysecretbrussels.com*.

THE AUTHOR

Derek Blyth has lived in Brussels for more than 20 years. He drinks coffee in Askam and Blomquists. He buys wine at Mig's. He cycles down the Rue de la Paix to buy croissants at Renard. He likes to eat mussels at Les Brassins and drink Poperings Hommelbier at L'Ultime Atome.

Formerly editor of the Brussels English-language weekly The Bulletin, he has written several books on the Low Countries, including *Brussels for Pleasure* and *Flemish Cities Explored*. He is cofounder of the discussion forum Café Europa and contributes a regular column on Brussels life to Eurostar's Metropolitan magazine. He created the website *www.mysecretbrussels.com* and tweets *@secretbrussels*.

In drawing up the lists, the author has taken advice from friends, family, journalists and local historians. He thanks Anna Blyth, Lucia Cabanova and Nathalie Piana for checking out places to go clubbing, Michel Verlinden and Pieter Vandoveren for restaurant suggestions, and Katrien Lindemans for shopping tips.

BRUSSELS:

overview

8 Sainctelette

Station Brussels Nord

9 Schaerbeek and Saint-Josse

2 Dansaert quarter

Central station

Anspachlaan

1 Central Brussels

4 European Quarter

7 Anderlecht

3 Sablon and Marolles

Station Brussels Midi

5 Louise, Ixelles and Uccle

6 Saint-Gilles and Forest

Map 1

CENTRAL BRUSSELS

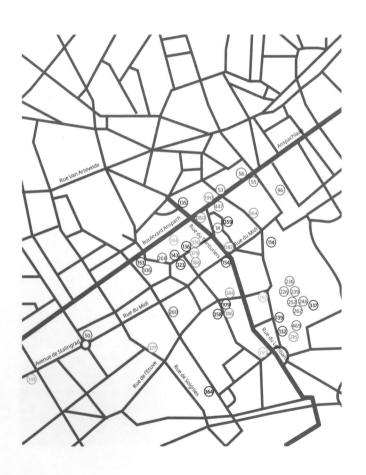

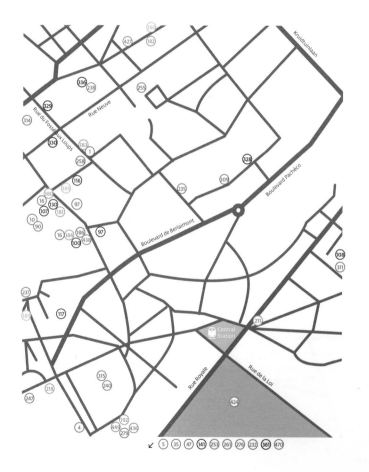

Map 2

DANSAERT QUARTER

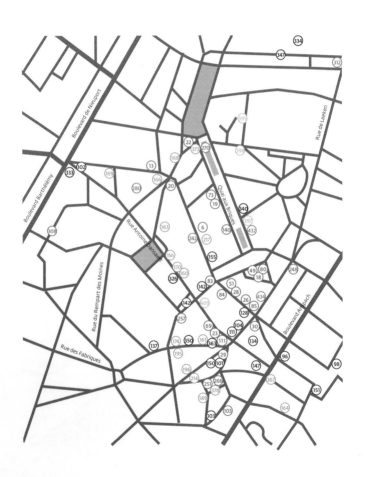

Map 3

SABLON *and* MAROLLES

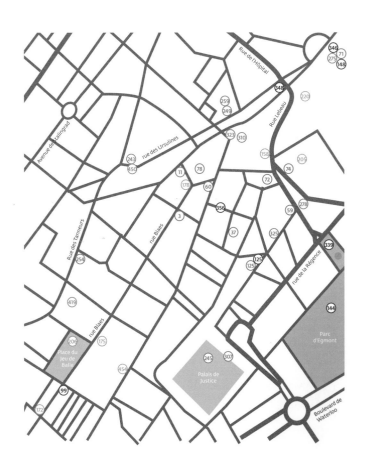

Map 4
EUROPEAN QUARTER

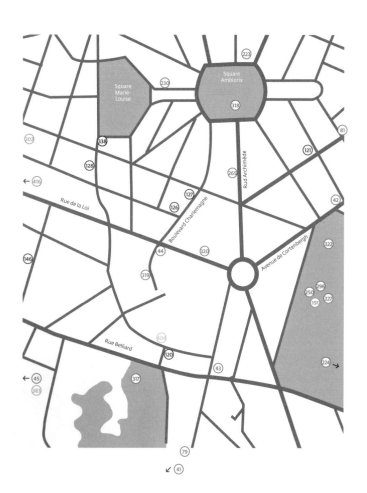

Map 5
LOUISE, IXELLES
and UCCLE

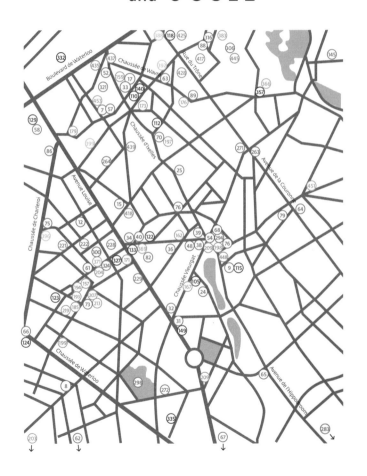

Map 6
SAINT-
GILLES

Map 7
ANDER-
LECHT

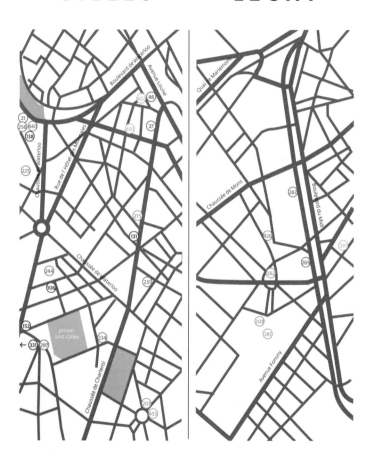

Map 8

SAINCTELETTE

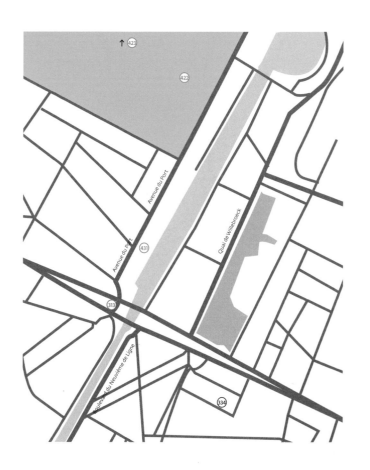

Map 9
SCHAERBEEK
and SAINT-JOSSE

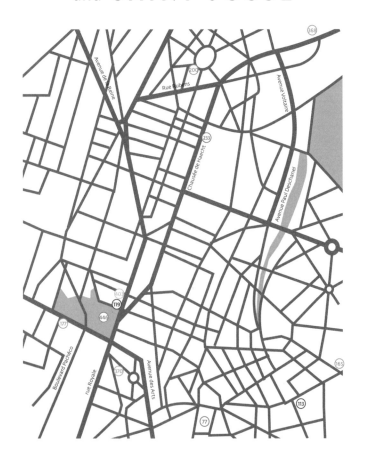

LES BRIGITTINES

95 PLACES
TO EAT GOOD FOOD

1 **BELGA QUEEN**

Rue Fossé aux Loups 32
Central Brussels ①
+32 (0)2 217 21 87
www.belgaqueen.be

Antoine Pinto created this grand restaurant in a former bank decorated with marble columns and a vaulted glass roof. The kitchen offers serious French cooking along with Belgian beer-based dishes. The toilets were the talk of the town when this place opened, but people are now reconciled to transparent cubicles that turn opaque when the door is closed.

2 **COOK & BOOK**

Place du Temps Libre 1
Woluwé-Saint-Lambert
+32 (0)2 761 26 00
www.cookandbook.com

Here is a place where you can eat lunch in one of nine beautiful bookshops. Each bookshop/restaurant has a different theme and decor: a Fiat 500 sits in the cookbook section, an Airstream is parked in the middle of the travel books, and novels hang from the ceiling in the literature shop. It's quite confusing, but it somehow works, a bit like Belgium.

3   L'IDIOT DU VILLAGE

**Rue Notre-Seigneur 19
Marolles** ③
+32 (0)2 502 55 82

You will never find The Village Idiot by chance. It's hidden down a narrow cobbled lane in the Marolles, not far from the antique shops. The dark interior has a cluttered feel, like the home of an elderly uncle. The chef's specialities include a rich rabbit stew flavoured with wine.

4   KWINT

**Mont des Arts 1
Central Brussels** ①
+32 (0)2 505 95 95
www.kwintbrussels.com

Named after the 16th century emperor Charles Quint, this beautiful brasserie has brought stylish dining to the Mont des Arts. With its sweeping views of the old town and hanging copper sculpture by Arne Quinze, this is one of the most spectacular places to eat in town. The cooking uses fine ingredients like caviar, truffles and smoked salmon.

5   MUSEUM CAFÉ

**Rue de la Régence 3
Central Brussels** ①
+32 (0)2 508 35 80
www.museumfood.be

The menu in the Museum Café, located in the 19th Museum of Fine Arts, was devised by Peter Goossens, one of the country's best chefs. It includes Belgian staples like vol-au-vent, and mussels and frites. It is self-service, so you may have to wait. The café opens its terrace in the summer months.

The 5 best restaurants to
EAT LIKE A BELGIAN

6 **VIVA M'BOMA**
Rue de Flandre 17
Central Brussels ②
+32 (0)2 512 15 93

Viva m'Boma ('long live grandmother') is located in a former tripe shop decorated with white tile walls. This is one of the best places in town for traditional Brussels dishes like meat balls served with tomato sauce, *stoemp* and, of course, tripe.

7 **LES BRASSINS**
Rue Keyenveld 36
Ixelles ⑤
+32 (0)2 512 69 99
www.lesbrassins.com

Located in the street where Audrey Hepburn was born, this is one of the best traditional brasseries in Brussels. Locals and Europeans find their way to this dingy back street to enjoy the hearty Belgian cooking, with specialities to sustain you through a cold winter night like *stoemp saucisse* (sausage and mashed potato) and *lapin à la kriek* (rabbit in beer sauce). The beer list includes some rare bottles.

8   LE TOUCAN BRASSERIE

Avenue Louis Lepoutre 1
Ixelles ⑤
+32 (0)2 345 64 78
www.toucanbrasserie.com

Here is a noisy, crowded French-style brasserie with friendly young staff and tasty cooking. You come here to eat familiar brasserie cooking like croquettes aux crevettes grises (North Sea shrimp croquettes) and jambonneau (a hefty knuckle of ham). The sister restaurant Toucan sur Mer up the road serves huge plates of seafood in a setting that evokes the French Atlantic coast.

9   LE VARIÉTÉS

Place Saint Croix 4
Ixelles ⑤
+32 (0)2 647 04 36
www.levarietes.be

A busy brasserie in a corner of the Flagey building with an interior designed in art deco style. The kitchen specialises in nostalgic Belgian cooking, like grilled chicken served with apple sauce.

10   AUX ARMES DE BRUXELLES

Rue des Bouchers 13
Central Brussels ①
+32 (0)2 511 55 98
www.auxarmesde-
bruxelles.be

Most Belgians will tell you to avoid the Rue des Bouchers, but it isn't that simple. Some of the restaurants are bad, but Aux Armes de Bruxelles is a classic Brussels place to eat. Founded in 1921, it focuses on Belgian dishes like mussels or water-zooi, served by waiters in crisp white jackets.

The 5 best restaurants for
BRUSSELS ATMOSPHERE

---

11 **LES BRIGITTINES**
Place de la Chapelle 5
Marolles ③
+32 (0)2 512 68 91
www.lesbrigittines.com

This stylish restaurant stands opposite the church where Pieter Bruegel is buried. The interior is decorated in a warm style, with mirrors, paintings and art nouveau lamps. The cook uses the best local ingredients, including Cantillon beer.

12 **CHOU DE BRUXELLES**
Rue de Florence 26
Ixelles ⑤
+32 (0)2 537 69 95

This friendly little restaurant in a quiet residential street is a good bet if you want traditional Belgian cuisine. The lamb is succulent, the frites are served in a paper cone, and the Zeeland mussels come with a choice of 30 different sauces. The place is always busy and staff occasionally struggle to cope with all the tables.

13 **HENRI**
Rue de Flandre 113
Central Brussels ②
+32 (0)2 218 00 08
www.restohenri.be

This bright and bustling brasserie in the heart of the Flemish quarter prepares delicious Belgian specialities such as shrimp croquettes and vol-au-vent. It gets very busy, so you need to book.

14 **PLATTESTEEN**
Rue du Marché
au Charbon 41 ①
Central Brussels
+32 (0)2 512 82 03

A friendly authentic Brussels brasserie in the gay area of the old town. The interior is wood-panelled, mirrored and a little bit aged, which is just how people like it. Perfect for steak-frites and a beer.

15 **LA VIGNE ET L'ASSIETTE**
Rue de la Longue Haie 51
Ixelles ⑤
+32 (0)2 647 68 03

In a quiet street off Avenue Louise, this simple neighbourhood restaurant has been around for several decades. It offers a choice of two menus, accompanied by outstanding wines selected by one of the country's best wine waiters.

11 LES BRIGITTINES

The 5 best restaurants for
FISH FROM
THE NORTH SEA

---

16 VINCENT

Rue des Dominicains 8
Central Brussels ①
+32 (0)2 511 26 07
www.restaurantvincent.
com

You have to squeeze through the kitchen to enter Vincent's dining room, where a dramatic 1905 tile mural shows fishermen battling in a high sea while another shows cows grazing in peaceful Belgian countryside. The elderly uniformed waiters bustle around in a very Belgian manner ensuring that everyone remains contented.

17 AU VIEUX BRUXELLES

Rue Saint-Boniface 35
Ixelles ⑤
+32 (0)2 503 31 11
www.auvieuxbruxelles.com

The oldest moules restaurant in Brussels, Aux Vieux Bruxelles opened its doors in 1882. Its frescos of Brussels scenes have faded with time, but it remains a lively place, with a mixture of locals and foreigners seated at small tables covered with red-checked tablecloths.

18 VISMET

Place Sainte-Catherine 23
Central Brussels ②
+32 (0)2 218 85 45

This sober wood-panelled fish restaurant has an open kitchen where you can see the chefs at work and a small pavement terrace that catches the evening sun. The sole meunière is close to perfect.

19 BIJ DEN BOER

Quai aux Briques 60
Central Brussels ②
+32 (0)2 512 61 22
www.bijdenboer.com

Most people miss this modest little fish restaurant. With its old stove and tiled interior, it looks more like a bar in rural Flanders. But Bij den Boer (At the Farmer) is one of the best fish restaurants in town, serving Belgian specialities like *croquettes aux crevettes*, *anguilles aux verts* and a sumptuous bouillabaisse of North Sea fish.

20 LA MARÉE

Rue de Flandre 99
Central Brussels ②
+32 (0)2 511 00 40
www.lamaree-sa.com

Not the easiest place to find, La Marée is a small fish restaurant behind the old fishmarket. Its customers are a mixture of regulars and tourists who have somehow been told to come here. The female chef cooks the perfect sole meunière or mussels fresh from the North Sea.

19 BIJ DEN BOER

The 5 best restaurants for
MEDITERRANEAN COOKING

---

21   LEONOR

Avenue de la Porte de
Hal 19
Saint-Gilles ⑥
+32 (0)2 537 51 56

The Gare du Midi neighbourhood is dotted with Spanish restaurants, but Leonor stands out from the crowd. This sober corner restaurant offers classic Spanish cooking with a modern touch, including an outstanding tapas menu in which one stunning dish follows another until you can eat no more.

22   STROFILIA

Rue du Marché aux
Porcs
Central Brussels ②
+32 (0)2 512 32 93

This exceptional Greek restaurant not far from the fish market occupies a former wine warehouse with 17th century vaulted brick cellars. The upstairs area was recently redecorated in a fun modern style, but the cellars have been left untouched. The perfect place to try spicy Greek *spentzotai* sausages and other *mezze* dishes.

23   LA KASBAH

Rue Antoine Dansaert 20
Central Brussels ②
+32 (0)2 502 40 26
www.lakasbah.be

Kasbah's dark interior stands out amid the cool design of Rue Dansaert. Here you can sink into thick cushions and feast on Moroccan couscous and tagines.

24 KIF-KIF

Square Biarritz 1
Ixelles ⑤
+32 (0)2 644 18 10

Kif-Kif's owners Yaëlle and Djiad have blended Moroccan and Jewish cooking traditions in this restaurant overlooking the Ixelles ponds. The waiters are charming and the secluded waterside terrace is enchanting on a summer evening.

25 L'OUZERIE

Chaussée d'Ixelles 235
Ixelles ⑤
+32 (0)2 646 44 49

Here is a good Greek restaurant where you are not surrounded by plaster statues of Gods and bunches of plastic grapes. Locals and Greek Eurocrats pack into this small restaurant to eat delicious dishes like grilled octopus, fried squid or the purée of split peas.

23 LA KASBAH

The 5 most exotic
ASIAN RESTAURANTS

---

26 **LITTLE ASIA**
Rue Sainte-Catherine 8
Central Brussels ②
+32 (0)2 502 88 36
www.littleasia.be

Quyên Truong Thi came to Belgium as a refugee. She now runs a cool little lounge restaurant which serves some of the best Vietnamese cuisine in the country. The waiters wear stylish costumes while the food is just sublime.

27 **PREMIER COMPTOIR THAI**
Chaussée de
Charleroi 39 ⑥
Saint-Gilles
+32 (0)2 537 44 47

This intimate restaurant serves delicious Thai food in a warm setting. The secluded back garden is one of the most romantic spots we know.

28 **HONG KONG DELIGHT**
Rue Sainte-Catherine 35
Central Brussels ②
+32 (0)2 502 27 80

A tiny Chinese restaurant that most people walk straight past. It may look like a simple snack bar, but this place serves some of the best Cantonese food in town.

29 **HONG HOA**
Rue du Pont de
la Carpe 18 ②
Central Brussels
+32 (0)2 502 87 14

It's easy to walk past this tiny Vietnamese restaurant close to Place Saint-Géry. It's run by one family, with father in the kitchen and two brothers and a sister serving the food. A good address for simple cooking.

30 **AU BON BOL**
Rue Paul Delvaux 9
Central Brussels ②
+32 (0)2 513 16 88

An authentic Chinese noodle house down a quiet street near the Bourse. The noodles are handmade as you wait, while the soups are delicious and filling.

The 5 best
JAPANESE
RESTAURANTS

---

31 KOKUBAN
Rue Vilain XIIII 55
Ixelles ⑤
+32 (0)2 611 06 22
www.kokuban.be

Located in a quarter dotted with Japanese restaurants, Kokuban is inspired by traditional ramen bars. Seated at pale wood tables in a sober interior, customers can eat delicious specialities such as *gyoza* (Japanese ravioli filled with chicken and vegetables) followed by ramen (large bowls of noodles and vegetables in a thin broth). Good for a quick lunch but not a place to linger.

32 IZAKA-YA
Chaussée de
Vleurgat 123
Ixelles ⑤
+32 (0)2 648 38 05

An authentic, rather basic, restaurant that is packed at lunchtime with Japanese office workers based in the neighbourhood. Squeeze in, if you can, and order the Mix Sashimi lunch menu, which includes fresh fish, rice, miso soup and all the tea you can drink.

33 YAMATO
Rue Francart 11
Ixelles ⑤
+32 (0)2 502 28 93

This tiny Japanese canteen off Place Saint Boniface barely holds 15 people. It is always full. You might have to wait 30 minutes, but it is worth it, especially for the ramen (noodles floating in a broth) served with dumplings.

34 KUSHI TEI OF TOKIO

Rue Lesbroussart 118
Ixelles ⑤
+32 (0)2 646 48 15
www.kushi-tei.com

Smart? Not really. But this little Japanese restaurant off Avenue Louise is always packed. Maybe it's the smiling chef behind the counter, who puts together delicious lunch menus that include soup, vegetables, meat or fish, and other delights, which he finishes off with a sprinkling of sesame seeds and a dash of sauce. One of the best lunch deals in the city.

35 RESTO POINT BAR

Rue du Pépin 39
Central Brussels ①
+32 (0)2 503 04 03
www.restopointbar.be

This cool modern restaurant was the talk of the town when it opened a few years ago. Locals raved about the cute pink décor, the innovative Asian fusion cooking and the concept of serving everything in glass jars. It's expensive and slightly weird, but fun to try once.

35 RESTO POINT BAR

The 5 best places for a
HEALTHY LUNCH

---

36 **SLURPS**
Rue Dautzenberg 7
Ixelles ⑤
+32 (0)2 647 47 38
www.slurps.be

Here is one of the best vegetarian restaurants in town. The food is prepared according to Indian Ayurvedic principles. You might have a long wait, but the food is fragrant and delicious.

37 **SOUL**
Rue Samaritaine 20
Central Brussels ③
+32 (0)2 513 52 13
www.soulresto.com

Two Finnish sisters run this cool little restaurant in a cobbled back street of the Marolles. The cooking is done without gluten, butter or cream. But the menu does have some meat and fish dishes, so not somewhere for strict vegetarians.

38 **TROP BON**
Chaussée de Vleurgat 1
Ixelles ⑤
+32 (0)2 640 40 57
www.tropbon.be

Two women run this cheerful urban canteen, which is decorated with bare wood floors and orange chairs. They offer slow food dishes listed on a blackboard, ranging from a simple soup or sandwich to a tasty dish of the day. Some dishes contain meat from bio farms.

39 DOLMA

Chaussée d'Ixelles 329
Ixelles ⑤
+32 (0)2 649 89 81
www.dolma.be

This friendly vegetarian restaurant close to Place Flagey serves vegan and vegetarian dishes, including a generous Tibetan-style buffet. The place has a bar, garden and health food shop.

40 FRESH COMPANY

Rue Lesbroussart 120
Ixelles ⑤
+32 (0)2 648 56 58
www.fresh-company.be

Mary Fehily, an Irish chef, creates healthy lunch dishes with a hint of the Mediterranean. The contemporary cooking is matched by a modern interior designed by Anne Derasse. Booking essential.

The 5 best places for lunch
IN THE EUROPEAN QUARTER

---

41 SCHIEVELAVABO
Chaussée de Wavre 344
European Quarter ④
+32 (0)2 280 00 83
www.leschievelavabo.
jourdan.be

A Schievelavabo in Brussels dialect is a squint washbasin, or someone not to be trusted. This restaurant can be trusted if you are simply looking for basic Brussels food and a moderate bill. The interior is decorated like an old Belgian café with wooden tables and enamel beer signs. Other branches in Uccle, Forest and Woluwé-Saint-Pierre.

42 FRESH & YOU
Avenue de
Cortenbergh 134
European Quarter ④
www.freshandyou.be

A superior lunch place with an Italian touch aimed at EU office workers. Sandwiches are made on the spot with good bread and fresh vegetables. The chocolate fondant is sublime.

43 EXKI FROISSART
Rue Froissart
European Quarter ④
www.exki.be

This branch of Exki next to the Justus Lipsius building is popular with EU office workers looking for a healthy alternative to canteen food. The sandwiches are tasty, salads are fresh, but the coffee is disappointing. It's expensive, but friendly and always busy.

44 RESIDENCE PALACE

Rue de la Loi 155
European Quarter ④
+32 (0)2 235 21 04
www.presscenter.org

Here is a very smart restaurant inside a gorgeous art deco building with a fountain in the lobby. You have to pick your way through a muddy construction site to get here, but it's worth it to enjoy the good-value lunch menu. Popular with journalists, it feels like a private club, especially when you order coffee in the intimate salon.

45 AMOR AMOR

Rue du Trône 13
European Quarter ④
+32 (0)2 511 80 33

On the edge of the EU quarter, this modest restaurant offers excellent Italian cooking using the freshest ingredients. Convenient for people based at the European Parliament, but too far perhaps for the European Commission crowd.

The 5 best places for
BURGERS

---

46 COOL BUN
Rue Berckmans 34
Saint-Gilles ⑥
+32 (0)2 537 80 02
www.cool-bun.be

This burger restaurant near Place Stéphanie attracts a cosmopolitan crowd. The Scandinavian interior and quotes hand-painted on the wall create a cool ambience. And the chef cooks up delicious burgers using the best ingredients. The frites are faultless and the beer list includes sublime Belgian brews.

47 COMICS CAFÉ
Place du Grand Sablon 8
Central Brussels ①
+32 (0)2 513 13 23
www.comicscafe.be

Here is a restaurant that serves big New York size burgers. It's a friendly, fun place located above a comic bookshop, with red checked tablecloths and comic illustrations on the walls.

48 LES SUPER FILLES DU TRAM
Rue Lesbroussart 22
Ixelles ⑤
+32 (0)2 648 46 60
www.superfillesdutram.com

Two women run this funky burger joint close to Place Flagey. The name refers to "those superwomen you see on the tram, who look as if their lives are perfect in every way". The Super Filles concoct delicious traditional burgers along with unusual versions involving grilled chicken or salmon, accompanied by chunky fries.

49 ELLIS GOURMET BURGER

Place Sainte-Catherine 4
Central Brussels ②
+32 (0)2 514 23 14
www.ellisgourmetburger.com

Six Belgian friends got together in 2011 with the aim of creating a decent US-style burger restaurant. The place has a cool, modern look, with nostalgic pictures from burger history on the walls. The burgers are made with the very best beef.

50 HOUTSIPLOU

Place Rouppe 9
Central Brussels ①
+32 (0)2 511 38 16
www.houtsiplou.be

A friendly little place on two levels with funky comic murals referring to Belgium's history. The burgers are tasty and frites come in a flower pot. A fun place to take kids.

49 ELLIS GOURMET BURGER

The 5 best places for
CHEAP EATS

51 **NOORDZEE**
Rue Sainte-Catherine 45
Central Brussels ②
www.vishandelnoordzee.be

The cheerful staff serve up delicious seafood at a long curved metal counter outside Noordzee fish shop. You choose from the list on the blackboard and give your name and the order is cooked up on the spot using the freshest seafood. We recommend the calamares à la plancha or a simple bowl of Véronique's fish soup, washed down with a glass of Chilean white wine.

52 **WOKÉ**
Avenue de la Toison
d'Or 17-20
Ixelles ⑤
www.woke.be

Here is a fun place to grab a bite before a film. Located opposite the UGC Toison d'Or cinema, Woké lets you put together your own wok dish out of vegetables, meat and fish. The food is cooked on the spot for you to eat in the upstairs canteen. You can also assemble a smoothie out of assorted fruits.

51 NOORDZEE

53 CHAOCHOW CITY

Boulevard Anspach 89
Central Brussels ①
+32 (0)2.512.37.56

No one would call Chaochow City sophisticated. The waitress takes your order before you have sat down. The food arrives barely 30 seconds later. You have a choice of two dishes of the day in this austere Chinese canteen. The lacquered pork (crispy on the outside and tender on the inside) is of unbeatable value.

54 FLAGEY OYSTER BAR

Place Flagey
Ixelles ⑤

The Sunday market on Place Flagey has become a place to meet friends over oysters and champagne. You can pick up half a dozen oysters for €6, a glass of something bubbly for €2 and perch on a stool. Possibly the most sophisticated snack in town.

55 CHEZ JEF ET FILS

Boulevard Anspach ①
Facing the Bourse
Central Brussels

The friendly Jef and his son sell steamy escargots (snails) from a cramped cabin parked on the pavement opposite the stock exchange. A plate of 12 escargots costs less than €5 at this Brussels institution.

The 5 best places for a
HEALTHY SANDWICH

---

56 AU SUISSE
Boulevard Anspach 73
Central Brussels ①
+32 (0)2 512 95 89
www.ausuisse.be

The oldest sandwich bar in Brussels was founded in 1873 by a Swiss woman called Madame Togni. The shop was given a modern streamlined upgrade in the 1930s, but has been left virtually untouched since then. You order a sandwich at one counter and then perch on a stool on the opposite counter to eat it.

57 L'EPICERIE
Rue Keyenveld 56
Ixelles ⑤
+32 (0)2 513 71 84

Monghton Tangton took over an old Ixelles grocery store in 2001 and transformed it into a lunchtime snack bar. He has kept the old shelves and added an assortment of ancient schoolroom furniture to create an antiquated Belgian atmosphere. The sandwiches are made with gently toasted ciabatta bread which is spread with homemade guacamole, basil leaves and prawns or Parma ham.

58 THERESE ET DOMINIQUE

Rue Dejoncker 23
Ixelles ⑤

This looks like a plain sandwich shop, but the queue at lunchtime goes out of the door. It's run by an Italian family who use good bread and fresh ingredients to create delicious sandwiches. One of the best is made with fried aubergine, sweet red peppers, tomatoes and mozzarella. The eating area is basic, but there is a secret garden at the back for summer days.

59 CLAIRE FONTAINE

Rue Ernest Allard 3
Sablon ③
+32 (0)2 512 24 10

The shelves in this delicatessen are crammed with jars of olive oil, French jams and sea salt. The interior is tiny, barely enough to hold two people. At lunchtime, a long line of customers stretches along the pavement, everyone waiting patiently for one of Claire's homemade sandwiches.

60 PICNIC

Place de la Chapelle 16
Marolles ③
+32 (0)2 503 63 23
www.traiteur-picnic.be

A pretty little sandwich bar in the Marolles where antique dealers rub shoulders with students. The sandwiches are freshly made with warm ciabatta bread and filled with whatever you fancy – anything from goat's cheese and honey to roast beef with aubergine. The upstairs room is a romantic space with ancient brick walls and a view of the Eglise de la Chapelle.

The 5 best
CAKE SHOPS

---

61 LES CAPRICES DU BAILLI
Rue du Bailli 75
Ixelles ⑤
+32 (0)2 538 79 93

This is a serious patisserie located in a 1900 art nouveau shop decorated with tiled floor, Empire mouldings and stained glass. The cakes come from the Debailleul bakery in Koekelberg. Admire the beautiful boxes and listen carefully as the slightly severe lady behind the counter tells you precisely how to serve the gateau you have selected.

62 LE SAINTE-AULAYE
Rue Vanderkindere 377
Uccle ⑤
+32 (0)2 345 77 85
www.saintaulaye.be

Established in 1986, this bakery takes its name from a little town in the Dordogne where the owner served as an apprentice baker. The cakes and tarts are gorgeous concoctions to liven up a dinner party, but this is also a place to pick up a simple baguette or a bag of croissants for breakfast.

63 MAISON RENARDY

Chaussée de Wavre 111B
Ixelles ⑤
+32 (0)2 514 30 17

This convivial family-run bakery in the heart of the African quarter looks a bit out of place, surrounded by shops selling hair extensions and companies shipping to Kinshasa. It was founded in 1912 when this was a prim bourgeois neighbourhood. Excellent for coffee, bread and croissants, or to pick up a little bag of homemade chocolates.

64 CONFEITARIA GARCIA

Avenue de
la Couronne 75
Ixelles ⑤
+32 (0)2 640 79 56
www.patisseriegarcia.be

This traditional Portuguese cake shop and bakery was opened in 1990 by Rui Manuel Garcia Borralho. The interior is designed to look like a sunny courtyard in Portugal, complete with splashing fountain, tiled roof and fake swallow nests. Melancholy Fado music plays in the background to complete the illusion. Here is the perfect place to try Pastel de Nata, a flaky pastry filled with custard.

65 LES TARTES DE FRANÇOISE

Avenue de
l'Hippodroom 75
Ixelles ⑤
+32 (0)2 640 88 41
www.tartes.be

A nondescript door on a busy street. You go in. A narrow corridor leads to a back room. A cook is pulling a lemon tart from a large oven. Welcome to Les Tartes de Françoise, where Belgians have been queuing for savoury quiches and sweet tarts since 1984. The company now has a branch in Manhattan's Hell's Kitchen district, but it all started in this secret place.

The 5 best places for
A SUNDAY BRUNCH

---

66 **GAUDRON**
Place Brugmann 3
Ixelles ⑤
+32 (0)2 343 97 90
www.gaudron.be

This Belgian delicatessen stands on a desirable square overlooked by Parisian-style apartments. It used to be an old-fashioned tea room where elderly Belgian women went with their ridiculous fluffy dogs, but the owners recently ripped out the old furniture and redecorated in a surprisingly cool style. It's now a very fashionable place with a range of brunch menus served at weekends from 7am to 5pm. You can order English breakfast (bacon and eggs), Continental breakfast (baguette and croissants) or a simple plate of pancakes.

67 **CAFÉ DE LA PRESSE**
Avenue Louise 493
Central Brussels ⑤

This cool new café with big glass windows, brown patterned wallpaper and vintage armchairs looks like a Fifties interior magazine advert. Located at the far end of Avenue Louise, it's too far from the office hubs to serve as weekday canteen, but it's the perfect place for a lazy weekend brunch, followed by a walk in the Bois de la Cambre.

68 **BELGA**
Place Flagey 18
Ixelles ⑤
+32 (0)2 640 35 08
www.cafebelga.be

The café on the ground floor of Flagey looks as if it has been around since the Thirties, but it was in fact created by Frédéric Nicolay just a few years ago. It's hard to find a table on Sunday mornings, when couples and young families head here for brunch after picking up a few things at the local market. You order at the bar, which is unusual in Belgium. Ask the barista for the wifi password if you need to check your emails.

69 LE PAIN QUOTIDIEN

Rue Dansaert 16
Central Brussels ②
+32 (0)2 502 23 61
www.lepainquotidien.be

Alain Coumont opened the first Pain Quotidien on Rue Dansaert back in 1990. People loved the big farmhouse table and the shelves stacked with round sourbread loaves, and the concept grew into a global brand, with branches in London, New York and Paris. It may not be so original any more, but the first branch on Rue Dansaert remains a lovely place for Sunday brunch.

70 L'AMOUR FOU

Chaussée d'Ixelles 185
Ixelles ⑤
+32 (0)2 325 73 53
www.lamourfou.be

This used to be a fashionable bar opposite Ixelles town hall. Then it closed. Now it's back in business with a slight American twist at the weekend when they offer brunch from noon to 5pm. The menu offers a choice of New York, Malibu, or London style. The best option is probably the New York with thick fluffy pancakes, fresh fruit and maple syrup.

The 5 best shops for
BELGIAN CHOCOLATES

---

71 LAURENT GERBAUD
Rue Ravenstein 2D
Central Brussels ③
+32 (0)2 511 16 02
www.chocolatsgerbaud.be

Laurent Gerbaud creates delicious little chocolates flavoured with exotic fruits and spices from the Far East. He sells them in a stylish shop opposite Bozar arts centre. The coffee bar sells good espresso with a single Gerbaud chocolate.

72 PIERRE MARCOLINI
Rue des Minimes 1
Sablon ③
+32 (0)2 514 12 06
www.marcolini.be

Pierre Marcolini started out in the 1990s with a small chocolate shop outside Brussels. He now has eight branches in Brussels and a further ten or so in other capital cities. He creates tiny square chocolates flavoured with hints of Moroccan pink pepper or Earl Grey tea, which he sells in stylish black boxes.

73 FREDERIC BLONDEEL
Quai aux Briques 24
Central Brussels ②
+32 (0)2 502 21 31
www.frederic-blondeel.be

Frederic Blondeel's chocolate shop and tea room is located in the heart of the fishmarket district. He makes elegant little chocolates that taste of ginger and basil. They are sold like Cartier diamond rings in little brown boxes placed in neat white carrier bags.

74 MARY

Rue Royale 73
Central Brussels ③
+32 (0)2 217 45 00
www.mary.be

This small shop, with its elegant rococo interior, is listed in the bestselling book *1,000 places to see before you die*. Founded soon after the end of the First World War, Mary supplies the Belgian royal family with its chocolates. A second shop recently opened in the Galeries Saint Hubert, but the Rue Royale shop is the one you should visit before you die.

75 ZAABAR

Chaussée de Charleroi 125
Saint-Gilles ⑤
+32 (0)2 533 95 80
www.zaabar.be

This chocolate shop looks more like a chemistry lab. The owner likes to experiment with strange flavours of chocolate, spiced with exotic ingredients like Ceylon cinnamon or Mekong peppermint. You can try little broken lumps laid out in bowls before placing your order. The shop also regularly organises chocolate-making workshops and guided tours.

73 FREDERIC BLONDEEL

The 5 best places for
PROPER BELGIAN FRITES

---

76 FRIT'FLAGEY
Place Flagey
Ixelles ⑤

It nearly vanished in early 2011, but a Facebook campaign saved this popular Ixelles frites stall from the bureaucrats. The owner Thierry had to abandon his old shack and move to a shiny new stall in a corner of the renovated square. But he still produces perfectly-fried frites which he serves in paper cones. It takes time. This is slow fast food. Be prepared to wait in a long line of customers, ranging from mothers with small children to hip Flemish journalists who work for TV Brussel.

77 FRITERIE MARTIN
Place Saint-Josse
Saint-Josse ⑨

It looked at one time as if the legendary friterie on Place Saint-Josse would vanish after Monsieur Martin retired. But the place has been taken over by Zoila Palma from Ecuador. She prepares the frites with as much care as her predecessor and serves them with a generous helping of mayonnaise perilously balanced at the top of the paper cone.

78 FRITUUR DE LA CHAPELLE

Place de la Chapelle
Marolles ③

A simple *frietkot* with two serving hatches next to the lovely Eglise de la Chapelle. The customers range from local school students to smart-suited antique dealers from the Sablon.

79 MAISON ANTOINE

Place Jourdan 1
European Quarter ④
www.maisonantoine.be

People say this is the best *frietkot* in Brussels. It's definitely the oldest – it was founded by Antoine Desmet back in 1948 in a shack left behind by the German army. It's also the most popular, which means you can easily wait in line for 30 minutes. You can eat your frites sitting on Café Bernard's terrace if you buy a drink.

80 PATRICK DE CORTE

Place Sainte-Catherine
Central Brussels ②

When Place Sainte-Catherine lost its *frietkot*, the locals launched a campaign to bring it back. So the gaudy pink rococo fairground van is now back on the square, serving steamy frites on cold evenings.

83 **CREMERIE DE LINKEBEEK**

The 5 best

FOOD SHOPS

---

81 JACK O'SHEA'S
Rue Titien 30
European Quarter ④
+32 (0)2 732 5351
www.jackoshea.com

Here is an authentic Irish butcher in the heart of the European Quarter. It's not cheap, but the quality is exceptional. Jack (not his real name) opened a second shop in London in 2006 that now provides Heston Blumenthal with his meat.

82 LE MARCHE DES CHEFS
Rue Lens 38
Ixelles ⑤
+32 (0)2 647 40 50

In Brussels, everything is a little bit hidden. So, as you would expect, the best food shop is located in a quiet back street. Belgians know to come here for the freshest fish shipped from Brittany, along with choice meat from the Limousin, lemons from Sicily and lamb reared on Basque hills. The trucks generally arrive with fresh food on Tuesdays.

**83 CREMERIE
DE LINKEBEEK**
Vieux Marché aux
Grains 4
Central Brussels ②
+32 (0)2 512 35 10

This traditional white tiled cheese shop has been around since 1902. It takes its name from the village of Linkebeek outside Brussels where the original owners grazed their cows. The current owners have revitalised the business while preserving its old charm. They now sell more than 120 cheeses, mostly Belgian and French, including the award-winning Achel Blue from Limburg and the almost vanished Fromage de Bruxelles. You can also buy milk in old glass bottles, as well as a New York style cheesecake.

84 **CHAMPIGROS**
Rue Sainte-Catherine 36
Central Brussels ②
www.champigros.be

Locals have been buying mushrooms and truffles from this specialist near Place Sainte-Catherine for more than 60 years. The shop sometimes has 20-30 varieties in stock.

85 **KAM-YUEN ASIAN MARKET**
Rue de la Vierge Noire 2
Central Brussels ②
+32 (0)2 511 48 68
www.kamyuen.be

This sprawling downtown food super-market stocks a vast range of products from China, Japan and India. Here you can find deep-fried crispy anchovies, large sacks of rice and frozen seafood shipped from the other side of the world.

The 5 best shops for
BEER AND WINE

---

86 **MIG'S WORLD WINES**
Chaussée de Charleroi 43
Saint-Gilles ⑤
www.migsworldwines.be

Miguel is a friendly Belgian who runs a cluttered wine shop close to Avenue Louise. Raised in Australia, Mig can talk for hours about the merits of different wines and persuade you to take home offbeat bottles from unknown vineyards. His Saturday morning tasting sessions can lead to some great discoveries.

87 **ROB**
Boulevard de la Woluwé 28
Woluwé-Saint-Pierre
+32 (0)2 761 01 66
www.rob-brussels.be

Rob is a large gourmet supermarket in the suburb of Woluwé with a basement stacked with some 1,800 different wines. Most of the stock comes from France, but you also find good Italian and Spanish wines. The wine department organises tastings on Saturdays.

88 **CRUSH WINE**
Rue Caroly 39
Ixelles ⑤
+32 (0)2 502 66 97
www.crushwine.eu

This little wine shop close to the European Parliament specialises in wine from Australia and New Zealand. The owners stock more than 200 different wines and organise free tasting sessions every month.

89 BEER MANIA

Chaussée de Wavre 174
Ixelles ⑤
+32 (0)2 512 17 88
www.beermania.be

Nasser Eftekhari runs a serious beer shop with over 400 labels on the shelves. Here is one of the few places in town where you can find Westvleteren, a Trappist beer from West Flanders voted by the influential website *RateBeer.com* as "the best beer in the world". The shop also sells its own beer called Mea Culpa which comes in a peculiar glass. There is a small tasting room at the back of the shop.

90 DELICES ET CAPRICES

Rue des Bouchers 68
Central Brussels ①
+32 (0)2 512 14 51
www.the-belgian-beer-tasting-shop.be

A tiny beer tasting shop down a quiet lane that you are unlikely to find by chance. The owner is friendly and passionate.

The 5 strangest items on a
BELGIAN MENU

---

91 STEAK AMERICAIN

This is not what an American would call a steak. It is raw minced beef served with a raw egg, mayonnaise and a sprinkling of raw onion. So now you have been warned.

92 BLOEMPANCH

A blood sausage filled with diced bacon and various spices.

93 MITRAILLETTE

A favourite with school students, the mitraillette, which literally means machine gun, is made with a half baguette, sliced in two, and piled with hamburger, frites, onions and a generous squirt of mayonnaise.

94 STOEMP

Mashed potatoes mixed with carrots, leeks, chicory or spinach. It is usually served with grilled sausage.

95 WATERZOOI

A delicious Flemish soup made from fish, mussels, shrimps, vegetables and cream. It can also be made from chicken.

BRASSERIE VERSCHUEREN

60 PLACES
FOR A DRINK

The 5 best bars to drink
LIKE A LOCAL

———

96 **CIRIO**
Rue de la Bourse 18
Central Brussels ②
+32 (0)2 512 13 95

The most beautiful café in Brussels, Cirio, has been around for over one hundred years. It takes its name from an Italian entrepreneur who invented a tomato-canning process and opened cafés and delicatessens in European cities. Cirio is one of the last survivors, a lovely period piece that manages to remain authentic. It's popular in the afternoon with elderly ladies who come here with their miniature dogs to drink white wine and spumante. In the early evening, the women go home to their Brussels apartments and a younger crowd takes over.

97 **À LA MORT SUBITE**
Rue Montagne-aux-
Herbes Potagères 7
Central Brussels ①
+32 (0)2 512 86 64

This spectacular café designed in 1910 by Paul Hamesse welcomes you with huge mirrors, marble columns and faded photographs of Jacques Brel. The waitresses are quite tart, the beer even more so. Mort Subite is hardly a hidden secret, yet it still has an authentic Brussels atmosphere.

98 À L'IMAIGE NOSTRE-DAME

**Impasse des Cadeaux 3
(off 8 Rue Marché aux
Herbes)
Central Brussels** ②
+32 (0)2 219 42 49

This bar at the end of a narrow white-washed passage feels more like a country inn. It opened in 1884 in a house that dates from the late 17th century. The bar consists of several snug rooms filled with antiques where locals chat or play a traditional Flemish pub game that involves tossing coins at a frog.

99 SKIEVEN ARCHITEK

**Place du Jeu de Balle 50
Marolles** ③
+32 (0)2 514 43 69

A likeable Flemish tavern buried under ivy on the square where the flea market is held. The interior is decorated with large murals of Brussels urban scenes and murky oil paintings. It opens before dawn, so the owners can sometimes seem a little weary come lunchtime.

100 MOKAFE

**Galerie du Roi 9
Central Brussels** ①
+32 (0)2 511 78 70

This traditional café is located in the city's most elegant arcade. The interior of wood panelling and green leatherette banquettes give it a literary feel. The perfect place for passing an hour with the newspapers on a rainy Sunday.

The 5
COOLEST BARS

---

101 **MAPPA MUNDO**
**Rue du Pont
de la Carpe 2-6
Central Brussels** ②
+32 (0)2 513 51 16
www.mappamundo.com

This downtown bar on two floors was designed by Frédéric Nicolay, as was the Roi des Belges on the opposite side of the street. It is always crowded, but you might manage to grab a table on the pavement terrace, or maybe, if you are very lucky, get one of the first-floor window booths looking down on the street.

102 **DE WALVIS**
**Rue Dansaert 209
Central Brussels** ②
+32 (0)2 219 95 32

Frédéric Nicolay made a bold move when he opened this bar at the shabby end of Rue Dansaert, looking across the canal to dark industrial Molenbeek. Yet this austere bare wood café is as popular as any Nicolay venture, attracting a mix of writers, fashionistas and locals.

103 **JAVA**
**Rue Saint-Géry 14
Central Brussels** ②
+32 (0)2 512 37 16

The long curved bar is the talking point here. Encrusted with coloured mosaics, it looks like something designed by Gaudi. This bar attracts a relaxed cosmopolitan crowd with its cocktails and Latin sounds.

104 **KAFKA**

Rue des Poissonniers 21
Central Brussels ②
+32 (0)475 980 539
www.cafekafka.be

This plain bar is decorated with a blurred photo of the gloomy Prague writer. Its austere interior makes it popular with the young Flemish artists and writers who live around here. It's a quiet, serious place during the day, where you could sit with a Belgian beer reading *The Trial*. But it gets more rowdy in the evening.

105 **DELECTA**

Rue Lannoy 2
Ixelles ⑤
+32 (0)2 644 19 49

Here is an odd, grungy place that was once a local grocery store. Frédéric Nicolay revamped it to create a modest place with wooden tables set in straight rows, 1970s floral wallpaper and an old iron stove. The food is interesting and Thursday nights are given over to DJ sessons.

The 5 bars with the
LONGEST BEER LISTS

---

106 CHEZ MOEDER LAMBIC
(300 BEERS)
Rue de Savoie 68
Saint-Gilles ⑥
+32 (0)2 544 16 99
Place Fontainas 8
Central Brussels ①
+32 (0)2 503 60 68
www.moederlambic.eu

The original Moeder Lambic lurks behind Saint-Gilles' town hall. It's a comfortable corner café with a deeply serious approach to beer drinking. It recently opened a new downtown branch on Place Fontainas with 46 different beers on tap. They serve plain, wholesome food, including sandwiches and quiches.

107 DELIRIUM
(2012 BEERS)
Impasse de
la Fidélité 4A
Central Brussels ①
+32 (0)2 514 44 34
www.deliriumcafe.be

This bar hidden at the end of an alley claims to stock one beer for every year of the Christian calendar. It is packed every evening with backpackers, students and visiting bands, all shouting at once in twelve different languages. It's great fun, but a bit frantic.

108 BIER CIRCUS
(200 BEERS)
Rue de l'Enseignement 57
Central Brussels ①
+32 (0)2 218 00 34
www.bier-circus.be

It takes a bit of effort to find this quiet bar in the Parliament district. You may wonder if it is worth it, but the beer list is exceptional, featuring some rare beers from small breweries in the Ardennes and rural Flanders.

109 **POECHENELLEKELDER**
(150 BEERS)
Rue de Chêne 5
Central Brussels ①
+32 (0)2 511 92 62

This bar stands directly opposite the famous Manneken Pis statue, so you would assume that it is a place to avoid. But, no, the owner has set his sights on creating a serious beer café. He is supported by locals who come here to drink good beer amid an eerie collection of dangling puppets.

110 **ULTIME ATOME**
(90 BEERS)
Place Saint Boniface 14
Ixelles ⑤
+32 (0)2 511 13 67
+32 (0)2 219 95 32

This lively brasserie in the heart of the African quarter appeals to everyone, from fashion students to couples who have been coming for the past 20 years. The eclectic beer list includes the elusive Poperings Hommelbier, a rare brew from West Flanders.

106 CHEZ MOEDER LAMBIC

The 5 best bars for

JAZZ AND BLUES

---

111 L'ARCHIDUC
Rue Antoine Dansaert 6
Central Brussels ②
+32 (0)2 512 06 52
www.archiduc.net

Ring the doorbell to enter. The doorman eventually admits you to this secretive cocktail bar built in 1937 in art deco style. The chrome detailing and balcony are now a bit faded, but the place is still one of the coolest places for jazz. Arrive at the right time, and someone will be playing the piano.

112 SOUNDS JAZZ CLUB
Rue de la Tulipe 28
Ixelles ⑤
+32 (0)2 512 92 50
www.soundsjazzclub.be

Back in the Eighties, Rosy and Sergio created this intimate jazz club in an Ixelles back street. Now a little worn, it's still a welcoming place with something happening most nights. Some big names in Belgian jazz have passed through this laid-back venue.

113 JAZZ STATION
Chaussée de
Louvain 193
Saint-Josse ⑨
+32 (0)2 733 13 78
www.jazzstation.be

Trains no longer stop at the Chaussée de Louvain station, but the 19th century Flemish Renaissance building is still standing next to the tracks. It was carefully restored in 2005 by the jazz-loving local mayor to create a striking modern jazz centre where emerging local talent is nurtured.

114 THE MUSIC VILLAGE
Rue des Pierres 50
Central Brussels ①
+32 (0)2 513 13 45
www.themusicvillage.com

This upmarket private jazz club occupies two 17th century houses near Grand' Place. It hosts some great jazz performers from Belgium and abroad.

115 LA SOUPAPE
Rue Alphonse
De Witte 26
Ixelles ⑤
+32 (0)2 649 58 88
www.lasoupape.be

This warm, intimate venue in a quiet street near Flagey has seats for just 50 people. It specialised in French chanson, but also hosts world music and jazz.

113 JAZZ STATION

The 5 best
HOTEL BARS

---

116 DOMINICAN LOUNGE BAR

Dominican Hotel
Rue Léopold 9
Central Brussels ①
+32 (0)2 203 08 08
www.thedominican.be

It used to be hard to find a decent place to drink around the opera house. Problem solved. The Dominican bar is a gorgeous space with high ceilings, chandeliers and comfy armchairs. If every last chair is taken, you can often find a table in a former cloister that looks out on a hidden garden.

117 LONGITUDE 4° 21'

Le Méridien Hotel
Carrefour de l'Europe 3
Central Brussels ①
+32 (0)2 548 42 11
www.lemeridienbrussels.be

A cool hotel lobby bar opposite Central Station with designer sofas and bookcases lined with real books. The hotel occasionally organises cultural events in the bar like book launches and readings.

118 LIBRARY BAR

Stanhope Hotel
Rue du Commerce 9
European Quarter ⑤
+32 (0)2 506 91 11
www.stanhope.be

This is one of the most civilised bars in the EU district. Tucked into a corner of the Stanhope Hotel's marble lobby, the Library Bar is decorated with leatherbound books and a painting of a dog above a blazing fire. There are newspapers to read while assorted nibbles come with the drinks.

119 SMOODS

Hotel Bloom
Rue Royale 250
Central Brussels ⑨
+32 (0)2 220 66 66
www.smoods.net

The seriously stylish Hotel Bloom has called in the designers to create a cool bar restaurant in the lobby. The place is divided into seven mood islands named passion, safari, bling-bling, library, bazaar, spring and flower power. The bar staff are relaxed and there are regular fashion events and DJ sets.

120 W XYZ BAR

Aloft Hotel
Place Jean Rey
European Quarter ④
+32 (0)2 800 08 88
www.aloftbrussels.com

Definitely the coolest place in the EU Quarter, the Aloft Hotel has a relaxed bar with pool table, funky lighting and a wooden deck with sofas for sitting out on summer evenings. Every Thursday, W XYZ hosts a DJ set that draws a young EU crowd.

The 5 best
WINE BARS

---

121 PIOLA LIBRI
Rue Franklin 66
European Quarter ④
+32 (0)2 736 93 91
www.piolalibri.be

A convivial Italian bookshop and wine bar on the edge of the European Quarter with three small rooms where you can order Italian wine and gather a small plate of free nibbles at the bar. The place gets lively in the early evening when it often hosts literary readings or concerts.

122 LE PETIT CANON
Rue Lesbroussart 96
Ixelles ⑤
+32 (0)2 640 38 34
www.lepetitcanon.be

This tiny wine bar occupies a corner building with space for only a few tables. So customers are more or less forced to sit at one of the pavement tables, sipping a glass of wine while tram 81 struggles up the hill.

123 OENO TK
Rue Africaine 29
Ixelles ⑤
+32 (0)2 534 64 34
www.oenotk.be

A hip wine shop and bar where the special offers are chalked up on huge blackboards. The owners have a relaxed approach to wine tasting that works well in this young cosmopolitan quarter.

124 WINERY

Place Brugmann 18
Ixelles ⑤
+32 (0)2 345 47 17
www.wineryonline.be

This serious little wine shop mainly stocks French wines selected by the Brussels expert Eric Boschman. When the weather is good, you can stop here after work for a glass of wine and a plate of salami.

125 CAFÉ PIXEL

Rue Ernest Allard 39
Sablon ③
+32 (0)2 502 20 84

This neat little wine bar in the heart of the antique district wins first prize for originality. The walls are covered with small square cushions in different colours that resemble the pixels in a digital image. An inspiring spot for a glass of wine.

125 **PIXEL**

The 5 best bars
TO HEAR NEW BANDS

---

126 **BAR DU MATIN**
Chaussée d'Alsemberg 172
Forest ⑥
+32 (0)2 537 71 59
bardumatin.blogspot.com

Frédéric Nicolay created this cool urban bar in his signature austere style. It immediately transformed a scruffy urban patch into a cool neighbourhood. Furnished with hard wooden chairs and big glass windows, the bar is relaxed during the day, while drawing late-night crowds on Thursdays, Fridays and Saturdays with a programme of jazz and DJ sets.

127 **BONNEFOOI**
Rue des Pierres 8
Central Brussels ②
www.bonnefooi.be

A relaxed bar with a Flemish feel that hosts DJ sessions just about every night. The place fills up in the late evening as people pour out of Ancienne Belgique and squeeze in here for a beer. The narrow mezzanine level can be booked for private parties.

128 **MONK**
Rue Sainte-Catherine 42
Central Brussels ②
+32 (0)2 503 08 80

A handsome old Brussels bar decorated with wood panelling, mirrors and a grand piano. The panelled back room has survived untouched, as has the cour, or back courtyard, where you find the toilets. Popular with the young Flemish crowd who hang out in this neighbourhood.

129 **LONDON CALLING**
Rue de Dublin 46
Ixelles ⑤
londoncallingdublin.word-press.com

This intimate music bar stands on a little square that has a village atmosphere. It has live concerts on several nights a week, but the music has to stop at midnight. Some people then head downstairs to the basement, where the partying continues.

130 **LAVA**
Rue Saint-Christophe
Central Brussels ②

This bar decorated with battered furniture and an ancient sofa opened only recently. It has become a popular place for the neighbourhood's chess players and hosts live jam sessions on Tuesdays.

The 5 best
COFFEE BARS

---

131 **PARLOR COFFEE**
Chaussée de
Charleroi 203
Saint-Gilles ⑥
+32 (0)474 42 13 25

The newest coffee bar in town has a friendly international feel. The interior is modern industrial style with plenty of places to sit around, including a quiet upper level, and stacks of glossy magazines to browse through. The espresso coffee comes from the roasting firm that supplies Or coffee shop.

132 **AKSUM COFFEE HOUSE**
Rue des Eperonniers 60
Central Brussels ①
+32 (0)484 07 76 95
www.aksumcoffeehouse.com

This cool coffee house moved in 2013 to a handsome old shop in central Brussels. The baristas make sublime espresso coffee using Ethiopian beans that are freshly roasted in a back room.

133 **NATURAL CAFFE**
Avenue Louise 196
Louise district ⑤
www.naturalcaffe.com

In this bright urban coffee bar, you can perch on stools watching trams rumble past the window. You pay at the cash desk, as in Italy, then sit down and wait while the barista prepares the order. The caffè espresso, served in a tiny Illy cup, is just about perfect.

134 OR COFFEE

Rue Orts 9
Central Brussels ②
+32 (0)2 511 74 00
www.orcoffee.be

Katrien Pauwels and her husband have created a laid-back coffee bar in downtown Brussels, decorated with exposed brick walls and small wooden tables. They serve coffee from their own coffee roasting factory in the Flemish village of Westrem. The room on the first floor is a quiet place to work.

135 BAR MOKA

Rue des Riches Claires 5
Central Brussels ①
www.barmoka.be

A tiny coffee bar in the Saint-Géry district with a Fifties feel. The German owner has built up a faithful clientele by serving excellent espressos using an authentic 1964 Italian Faema E61. A pity the opening hours are erratic.

132 AKSUM COFFEE HOUSE

The 5 most
ROMANTIC CAFÉS

━━━━━━━━━━

136 **LE CERCLE DES VOYAGEURS**
Rue des Grands
Carmes 18
Central Brussels ①
+32 (0)2 514 39 49
*www.lecercledesvoyageurs.
com*

This striking café located in a historic 17th century town house is something of a secret, despite being located no more than 50 steps from the Manneken Pis. The bare wood floor, worn-out armchairs and luxuriant potted plants create a wistful mood, like a colonial club in a far-off land.

137 **AM SWEET**
Rue des Chartreux 41
Central Brussels ②
+32 (0)2 513 51 31

A lovely cluttered tea room with several little rooms furnished with round metal tables, like a Parisian café. A narrow spiral staircase leads to the upper floor where couples can hide away from the world. The friendly owner An-Marie serves excellent teas by Mariage Frères of Paris and sublime chocolates by Laurent Gerbaud. The resident dog Cézanne completes the charm.

138 LA PORTEUSE D'EAU

Avenue Jean Volders 48
Saint-Gilles ⑥
+32 (0)2 537 66 46
www.laporteusedeau.be

Named after a nearby statue of a water carrier, La Porteuse d'Eau is a café on two floors with stained glass windows and a beautiful spiral staircase. Victor Horta, you might ask? It's actually a loving imitation, although it lies at the end of a row of genuine art nouveau houses. La Porteuse lies off the beaten track, so this idyllic corner café remains virtually unknown to anyone except the locals. The upper floor is the perfect spot for a quiet conversation over a rare beer.

139 GOUPIL LE FOL

Rue de la Violette 22
Central Brussels ①
+32 (0)2 511 13 96

This is a strange rambling place with mouldering sofas and stacks of old books. Some find it a bit too bohemian (it is rumoured to be a former brothel), but others love the warren of secret nooks and moody French music. Open until the early hours.

140 COMPTOIR FLORIAN

Rue Saint Boniface 17
Ixelles ⑤
+32 (0)2 513 91 03
www.comptoirflorian.be

This tiny tea room is squeezed into the back of a narrow art nouveau building designed by Ernest Blérot. The owner at the last count stocked more than 230 varieties of tea.

The 5 best terraces for
SITTING IN THE SUN

---

141 BELVUE MUSEUM
Place des Palais 7 /
Place Royale
Central Brussels ①
+32 (0)2 545 08 09
www.belvue.be

The BELVue Museum, once a grand hotel, has a secret enclosed courtyard where you can eat lunch sitting at a metal table under ancient trees. The self-service café offers healthy sandwiches and excellent salads produced by Green Attitude.

142 DE MARKTEN
Place du Vieux Marché
aux Grains
Central Brussels ②
+32 (0)2 513 98 55
www.demarkten.be

This stark white café is attached to the Flemish cultural centre De Markten. The café has a huge terrace on the square with tables shaded by ancient trees. It even puts out a few deckchairs in the summer. Perfect for a drink in the late afternoon sunshine.

143 AU SOLEIL
Rue du Marché
au Charbon 86
Central Brussels ①
+32 (0)2 513 34 30

This corner bar has kept the name and advertising signs from the days when it was a tailor's shop. It is now a fashionably bare café in a pedestrianised street with a generous supply of folding metal tables and chairs to benefit from the sunny location.

144 L'ORANGERIE DU PARC D'EGMONT

Parc d'Egmont
Sablon ③
+32 (0)2 513 99 48
www.restauration-nouvelle.be

Here is one of the loveliest terraces in the city. It belongs to L'Orangerie, a whitewashed building that laid abandoned and forgotten in the Egmont Park for many years. It is an attractive restaurant with a large outdoor terrace where you can sit under ancient trees in the dappled shade.

145 LA TERRASSE

Avenue des Celtes 1
Etterbeek
+32 (0)2 732 28 51
www.brasserielaterrasse.be

Here is a traditional Brussels café with an interior decorated with dark wood and mirrors, and a lovely pavement terrace enclosed by a thick hedge. The food is quite decent and the people who work here are unusually friendly.

144 L'ORANGERIE DU PARC D'EGMONT

The 5 best cafés for
FREE WIFI

---

146 **KARSMAKERS**
Rue des Trèves 20
Ixelles ④
+32 (0)2 502 02 26
www.karsmakers.be

Jyrki Karsmakers' coffee bar serves excellent espresso coffee in a bright modern interior opposite the European Parliament. The back room is especially appealing, with its big pine table, comfortable armchairs, coat hooks and toy boxes. The shady back garden is one of the most idyllic outdoor spots in the European Quarter.

147 **EXKI BOURSE**
Place de la Bourse 2
Central Brussels ②
www.exki.be

Every branch of Exki has free wifi. The stylish two-floor branch opposite the Bourse is one of the most spacious. In keeping with Exki's eco agenda, the colourful wall tiles on the ground floor come from demolished buildings, the fabrics come from recycled clothes, and the round tables on the first floor incorporate recycled stair bannisters.

148 **NATURAL CAFFE MONT DES ARTS**
Rue Mont des Arts 20
Central Brussels ③
www.naturalcaffe.com

A smart café in the Mont des Arts quarter, with a bright interior like a Fifties milk bar. Slightly off the beaten track, this is a quiet place to catch up on emails while sipping a creamy Illy coffee.

149 **EXKI BLUE TOWER**
Avenue Louise 326
Louise district ⑤
+32 (0)2 521 72 55
www.exki.be

This airy branch of Exki is easy to locate at the foot of the Blue Tower skyscraper, midway down Avenue Louise. The interior gets lots of light from the huge windows, while cool jazz often plays in the background. Head for the comfortable black armchairs at the back for a quiet place to check your emails.

150 **CAFÉ ZEBRA**
Place Saint-Géry 34
Central Brussels ②
+32 (0)2 511 09 01

A cool café facing the Halles Saint-Géry where you will find young Flemish laptop nomads sit at little round tables working through their emails.

The 5 best
L O C A L   B E E R S
and where to drink them

———————

151 **CANTILLON GEUZE**
A LA BÉCASSE
Rue de Tabora 11
Central Brussels ②
+32 (0)2 511 00 06

The first sip comes as a shock, but this classic Brussels sour beer may gradually win you over. It's brewed in an authentically old Brussels brewery down by the Midi Station using a traditional process that goes back centuries. It's sometimes called the Champagne of beers, yet Cantillon is sold in less than a dozen Brussels bars.

152 **ZINNEBIR**
BAR DU MATIN
Chaussée d'Alsemberg 172
Forest ⑥
+32 (0)2 537 71 59

This light Belgian ale with a hint of hops is gaining a following in Brussels, partly due to the beautiful label. It is brewed by the Brasserie de la Senne, which launched in rural Flanders but recently moved to industrial Molenbeek.

153 **DRIE FONTEINEN SCHAERBEEKSE KRIEK**
MOEDER LAMBIC
Place Fontainas 8
Central Brussels ①
+32 (0)2 503 60 68

An outstanding beer from a small lambic brewery in the village of Beersel, just east of Brussels. Served in a tumbler, it's a sour, complex beer that gets its flavour from the cherries added to the barrel.

154 LINDEMANS KRIEK CUVEE RENÉ

NÜETNIGENOUGH
Rue du Lombard 25
Central Brussels ①
+32 (0)2 513 78 84
www.nuetnigenough.be

Here is an excellent Kriek from an old family brewery in the Flemish village of Vlezenbeek. A sour beer with a deep red colour, it makes the perfect summer drink.

155 OUDE GEUZE OUD BEERSEL

ROSKAM
Rue de Flandre 9
Central Brussels ②
+32 (0)2 503 51 54
www.cafe-roskam.be

When the 19th century Oud Beersel brewery, located just south of Brussels, closed down in 2002, it looked like the end of the road for a distinctive lambic beer. But two young enthusiasts have revived the business and scooped several international awards for their outstanding geuze, including "world's best geuze" at the 2011 World Beer Awards.

152 BAR DU MATIN

65 PLACES TO SHOP

The 5 most inspiring
BRUSSELS DESIGNERS

---

156 Y-DRESS
Rue Dansaert 102
Central Brussels ②
+32 (0)2 502 69 81

Aleksandra Paszkowska designs a range of reversible clothes that are fun to wear. You can buy a skirt that turns into a dress, or a towel that converts into a beach dress. She has also developed some smart ideas for cycle wear and clothes for future mothers.

157 MAIS IL EST OÙ LE SOLEIL?
Rue Simonis 55
Ixelles ⑤
+32 (0)2 538 82 77
www.ousoleil.com

The Brussels fashion store *Mais il est où le soleil?* (But where is the sun?) was founded in 1998 by Belgians Laurence Everard and Valerie Pollet. Here you find bright, romantic clothes that combine flowing fabrics and delicate colours. Perfect for a summer party, as long as the sun shows.

158 ELVIS POMPILIO
Rue Lebeau 67
Sablon ③
+32 (0)2 512 85 88
www.elvispompilio.com

He used to be everywhere. Then he vanished. Now Pompilio is back in Brussels selling his eccentric hats. But he's keeping a low profile. No big shop. Just an atelier close to the Sablon, open three days a week.

159 NINA MEERT

Place Saint-Boniface 1
Ixelles ⑤
+32 (0)2 514 22 63
www.ninameert.be

Brussels designer Nina Meert sells romantic clothes in an elegant Art Nouveau shop. She grew up in Paris, but moved to Brussels in the 1970s. She creates unique dresses and wedding gowns using beautiful fabrics. Her clothes are sold in Harrods and worn by French film stars such as Isabelle Adjani and Isabelle Huppert.

160 ANNEMIE VERBEKE

Rue Dansaert 64
Central Brussels ②
+32 (0)2 511 21 71
www.annemieverbeke.be

The Flemish designer Annemie Verbeke creates clothes in a sober, somewhat melancholy style. Her aim is to create wearable styles for working women.

The 5 coolest
FASHION SHOPS

161 HUNTING & COLLECTING
Rue des Chartreux 17
Central Brussels ②
+32 (0)2 512 74 77
*www.huntingandcollecting.
com*

Niels Radtke and Aude Gribomont opened one of the most inspiring shops in Brussels in early 2010. As the name says, they hunt and collect an eclectic and edgy assortment of clothes, books and objects. They also exhibit art in the basement, publish a magazine and hold the occasional event.

162 RESERVOIR SHOP
Rue Lesbroussart 43A
Ixelles ⑤
www.rsrv.be

This store and gallery near Place Flagey has an eclectic selection of streetwear, magazines and accessories. Open on Sundays but closed on Mondays.

163 MAPP
Rue Léon Lepage 5
Central Brussels ②
+32 (0)2 551 17 67
www.thisismapp.com

A small concept store that stocks an diverse collection of clothes, magazines, CDs and objects. You can find gorgeous paper by Commune de Paris and cool knitwear by Henrik Vibskov. You may also discover an inspiring magazine or a CD you will play again and again.

164 MR EGO

Rue des Pierres 29
Central Brussels ②
+32 (0)2 502 47 87
www.mr-ego.be

A fun place to hunt for quirky clothes by brands like Pharmacy Industry and Etnies. It's also a good place to check posters and fliers for upcoming concerts.

165 SMETS

Chaussée de Louvain 650
Schaerbeek ⑨
+32 (0)2 325 12 30
www.smets.lu

Here is an exciting new concept store to hunt for cool clothes, design, art, jewellery and food. After starting in Luxembourg, Smets has arrived in Brussels. Not in a fashionable district, but on a busy road lined with car showrooms. It's worth the trek to see the interior mix of raw concrete, bright fabrics and cool music. There is also a bar and a restaurant.

The 5 most original shops for
BELGIAN FASHION

---

166 MAISON MARTIN MARGIELA

Rue de Flandre 114
Central Brussels ②
+32 (0)2 223 75 20
www.maisonmartinmargiela.com

No name. No nothing. The reclusive Antwerp designer Martin Margiela likes to keep a low profile. His Brussels store occupies an old corner building that has been painted white and decorated with cryptic letters. Buying something here is close to a religious experience. Ring the bell and wait to be admitted to the sanctuary.

167 ISABELLE DE BORCHGRAVE

Chaussée de Vleurgat 73
Ixelles ⑤
www.isabelledeborchgrave.com

Isabelle de Borchgrave is a Brussels artist and designer who creates extraordinary dresses entirely out of paper. Her studio, a beautiful two-floor space overlooking a minimalist garden, is oddly located at the back of a gloomy concrete car park. Here she shows off her creations and works by her favourite artists.

168 LE FABULEUX MARCEL DE BRUXELLES

Rue du Marché aux Porcs 8
Central Brussels ②
+32 (0)2 201 03 61
www.fabuleuxmarcel.com

This Belgian fashion brand has revived the plain white T-shirt worn by French hunks in old 1950s movies (known as *le marcel*). The shop interior is furnished with spiky Expo 58 tables that echo the brand's period identity.

169 CLJP ORIGINALS

Rue de la Clé 5
Central Brussels ②
+32 (0)2 219 17 93
www.cljp-originals.com

Carine Lauwers and her partner Jan Pieter de Kok have opened a shop in a beautifully restored former printing shop. It's an exclusive place, a little bit hidden, where individual dresses or jackets hang amid contemporary art. The clothes are made to measure in the workshop at the back.

170 CARINE GILSON

Rue Dansaert 87
Central Brussels ②
+32 (0)2 289 51 47
www.carinegilson.com

The Belgian designer Carine Gilson has a small atelier in Brussels where she creates fragile lingerie from delicate French silk and lace. She sells her hand-crafted pieces in a beautiful minimalist boutique.

The 5 best
VINTAGE SHOPS

───────────

171 LES ENFANTS D'EDOUARD

Avenue Louise 175–177
Ixelles ⑤
+32 (0)2 640 42 45
www.lesenfantsdedouard. com

Is this the right address? The splendid entrance hall decorated with a large mural of Brussels seems far too grand for a second-hand shop. Yet Les Enfants d'Edouard has been selling women's designer clothes at sharply reduced prices in this grand town house for several decades. The men's shop, a little less grand, is next door.

172 BERNARD GAVILAN

Rue Blaes 146
Marolles ③
+32 (0)2 502 01 28
www.bernardgavilan.com

Bernard Gavilan's little vintage shop close to the flea market is filled with fun stuff from the past, including shoes, handbags and big sunglasses.

173 LOOK 50

Rue de la Paix 10
Ixelles ⑤
+32 (0)2 512 24 18

A defunct juke box sits in the entrance of this vintage shop on the lively Rue de la Paix. They sell summer dresses, shoes and sunglasses last worn on a summer day thirtysomething years ago, as well as quirky 1960s lamps that until recently were probably gathering dust in a Belgian attic.

174 GABRIELE VINTAGE

Rue des Chartreux 27
Central Brussels ②
+32 (0)2 512 67 43
www.gabrielevintage.com

Look for the mannequin on the pavement dressed in fluorescent clothes. You've found Gabriele Vintage, whose German owner, Gabriele Wolf, arrived in Brussels as a costume designer but ended up running a shop full of flamboyant clothes. Her passion is hats, but she also sells 1920s cocktail dresses and platform shoes salvaged from the 1970s.

175 FOXHOLE

Rue des Renards 6
Marolles ③
+32 (0)477 20 53 36
www.foxholeshop.com

A well organised vintage shop near the flea market filled with funky clothes and bright accessories from the 1950s to the 1980s. Good for vintage shoes, trilby hats and psychedelic shirts. A second shop at Rue des Riches Claires 4 has a more limited range.

175 FOXHOLE

The 5 most
UNUSUAL SHOPS

---

176 DEMEULDRE
Chaussée de Wavre 141
Ixelles ⑤
+32 (0)2 511 93 73
www.demeuldre.com

This splendid porcelain shop stands on a rather scruffy Ixelles street. You may not even notice it. But stand back to admire the ornately tiled façade designed in 1905 and then, if you dare, step inside. Almost nothing has changed here in a century. Ask nicely and you can take a look at the tiny museum upstairs and the workshop where craftsmen repair precious broken plates.

177 PHARMACIE BOTANIQUE
Boulevard du Jardin
Botanique 36
Central Brussels ⑨
+32 (0)2 217 29 70

Belgian pharmacies are curious places where people head at the slightest hint of a sniffle to buy a full range of medicines from a lady in a white coat. They are splendid places to visit, none more so than this wood-panelled corner shop dating from 1911. The busts of Socrates and Hippocrates sit in niches, surrounded by cough remedies and painkillers.

178 STEFANTIEK

Place de la Chapelle 6/
Rue Blaes 63
Marolles ③
+32 (0)2 540 81 41
www.stefantiek.be

Anyone hunting for odd antiques should take time to poke around Stefantiek's two cluttered shops. Here you can find almost anything, from stone angels that once decorated a Belgian castle to an authentic fairground carousel.

179 SENTEURS D'AILLEURS

Place Stéphanie 1A
Ixelles ⑤
+32 (0)2 511 69 69
www.senteursdailleurs.com

Here is one of Europe's most stunning perfume shops. Founded by Pierre Donie after he lost his job, it sells exclusive perfumes like Penhaligon's and Maître Parfumier et Gantier in a beautiful shop that looks like a library. Next door, the family sells luxury cosmetics in a clinical white interior.

180 MAISON PHILIPPE

Boulevard Anspach 144
Central Brussels ①

This wig shop has barely changed since it was established in 1899. It still has an enamel sign on front promising "English spoken" and a window full of spooky heads fitted with dusty wigs.

178 STEFANTIEK

The 5 best
BOOKSHOPS

---

181 TROPISMES
Galerie des Princes 11
Central Brussels ①
+32 (0)2 512 88 52
www.tropismes.be

This beautiful bookshop occupies a former restaurant in a 19th century arcade. The ornate ceilings and high mirrors are still in place, creating a spectacular setting for browsing. Most of the books are in French, but they have a small section of English books next to the staircase.

182 WATERSTONES
Boulevard Adolph Max 71
Central Brussels ①
+32 (0)2 219 27 08

Originally a branch of WH Smith's, this English-language bookshop was founded in 1921. Now owned by Waterstones, the shop has thick carpets, knowledgeable staff and an inspiring range of books, magazines and newspapers. The neighbourhood, unfortunately, is not as smart as it was back in 1921.

183 STERLING
Rue du Fossé aux Loups 38
Central Brussels ①
+32 (0)2 223 62 23
www.sterlingbooks.be

This English-language bookshop near the opera house has a strong fiction section, a good collection of books on Brussels and a wide range of magazines.

184 LIBRAIRIE SAINT HUBERT

Galerie du Roi 2
Central Brussels ①
+32 (0)2 511 24 12
www.librairie-saint-hubert.com

A sumptuous art bookshop with a dark wood interior located in the Saint Hubert arcade. Contemporary art exhibitions are held in a small back room.

185 NIJINSKY

Rue du Page 15
Ixelles ⑤
+32 (0)2 539 20 28

A sublime secondhand bookshop located in the rambling ground floor rooms of two connected town houses. Named after the famous Russian dancer, Nijinsky stocks an eclectic range of books and art magazines. Most books are in French, but a small collection of English fiction is found in an alcove at the back.

The 5 best

INDEPENDENT RECORD STORES

---

186 ARLEQUIN

Rue du Chêne 7
Central Brussels ①
+32 (0)2 514 54 28
www.arlequin.net

This den of retro music near the Manneken Pis statue takes you back to the golden age of vinyl records in arty sleeves. The owners have squirrelled away a disparate stock of 1960s rock, moody French chanson, film scores, disco, electro, indie rock and rare stuff you will find nowhere else. A second branch in Saint-Gilles puts the focus on reggae, classical and world music.

187 HORS-SERIE

Rue du Midi 67
Central Brussels ①
+32 (0)2 534 79 59

This well-organised music shop on two floors has an eclectic collection of CDs, vinyl records, DVDs and comic books. The jazz section is enormous, while you can also hunt through inspiring selections of techno, chanson and world music.

188 VEALS & GEEKS

Rue des Grands
Carmes 8
Central Brussels ①
+32 (0)2 511 40 14
www.vealsandgeeks.com

Are you hunting for classic French chanson or the definitive guide to Italian Prog? Here is the place. In this eclectic secondhand store, you can find Jeff Potter's *Cooking for Geeks* alongside LPs from the Eighties and video games.

189 DOCTOR VINYL

Rue de la Grande Ile 1
Central Brussels ②
+32 (0)2 512 73 44

Here is an eclectic little shop in the cool Saint-Géry quarter, where local DJs and vinyl junkies hunt among the stock for rare recordings.

190 CAROLINE MUSIC

Boulevard Anspach 101
Central Brussels ①
+32 (0)2 502 10 83
https://www.facebook.com/carolinemusic.bsides

Music fans were thrilled when this record shop reopened in 2013. Now located opposite Ancienne Belgique, Caroline is back in business selling rare pop, indie and techno, as well as French chanson. It can also provide tickets for major concerts and festivals across the land.

The 5 best shops for
UNUSUAL GIFTS

191 PLASTER CAST WORKSHOP

Parc du Cinquantenaire
European Quarter ④
+32 (0)2 741 72 94
www.kmkg-mrah.be

Here is somewhere for a truly unusual gift. Located at the back of the Musée du Cinquantenaire, the workshop was founded by Léopold II to create replicas of classical sculptures. It now has row upon row of plaster cast figures, ranging from large statues to tiny cats from Egyptian tombs. Many are on sale in the shop.

192 BOZARSHOP

Rue Ravenstein 15
Central Brussels ①
+32 (0)2 514 35 05
www.bozarshop.com

This cool art shop attached to Bozar was designed by the Brussels architect Pierre Lhoas. It is stocked with T-shirts, creative toys, art books, DVDs of forgotten films, rare CDs, hard-to-find art magazines and some very strange Belgian postcards.

193 ROSE

Rue de l'Aqueduc 56
Ixelles ⑤
+32 (0)2 534 98 08
www.roseshop.be

A corner shop filled with colourful notebooks, stationery and gadgets. How about a Pantone mug in a vivid tone of green, or a sweet laptop case, or maybe a pink cuckoo clock?

194 ZAO

Rue du Bailli 96
Ixelles ⑤
+32 (0)2 534 38 32
www.zaodeco.be

A friendly shop filled with odd things that no one really needs, like funny Japanese gadgets, retro Diana cameras, silly fridge magnets and sublime notebooks designed by Cavallini & Co of San Francisco.

195 TOIT

Rue des Chartreux 46
Central Brussels ②
+32 (0)2 503 33 38
www.toit-bruxelles.be

This quirky shop sells gifts that appeal to the eclectic tastes of cool Brussels shoppers. In a pastel-coloured interior evoking Expo 58, you find pink cushions, old kitchen scales and stacks of tinned seafood.

192 BOZARSHOP

The 5 best
BIKE SHOPS

---

196 VELODROOM
Rue Van Artevelde 41
Central Brussels ②
+32 (0)2 513 81 99
www.velodroom.net

A friendly bike shop near Place Saint-Géry with young Flemish staff who know their stuff and can explain it in six languages. The shop specialises in solid Belgian urban bikes made by firms like Achielle, which are ideal machines for the daily commute. They also sell Brompton folding bicycles, which are popular with train commuters, though tough to ride up the city's steep hills, as well as cute wooden bikes for kids.

197 BLUE BICYCLE
Place Fernand Cocq 18
Ixelles ⑤
+32 (0)2 512 39 69

A well-run shop stocked with serious city bikes by Belgian and German brands. The owner has some useful tips on safe cycling in Brussels.

198 VAINQUEUR BICYCLES
Place Flagey 32
Ixelles ⑤
www.vainqueur.be

Here is a cool urban bike shop that specialises in fixed-gear city bikes with a bare minimum of parts to go wrong. They also sell a few secondhand bikes and carry out repairs in a very limited space.

199 FIXERATI

Rue du Page 88
Ixelles ⑤
+32 (0)2 534 11 21
www.fixerati.be

Hidden behind a garage door on the Rue du Page, this bike shop is not the easiest place to find. Nor are the opening hours particularly helpful. But they sell smart new racing bikes in every colour, plus locks, books and accessories.

200 VELO-CITE

Place Colignon 13-15
Schaerbeek ⑨
+32 (0)2 241 36 35
www.velocite.be

This bike shop occupies two corner shops opposite Schaerbeek's monumental town hall. The stock includes mountain and city bikes, as well as some secondhand models. They also rent and repair.

196 VELODROOM

The 5 best
NEWSAGENTS
open on a Sunday

---

201 CANDIDE

Place Brugmann 1
Ixelles ⑥
www.librairiecandide.be

This bookshop on Place Brugmann was recently transformed into a bright contemporary space by the Brussels architects Lhoas & Lhoas. They stock an excellent selection of international newspapers and magazines, including British Sunday newspapers. Once you have picked up a paper, sit down in Gaudron next door and order their petit déjeuner.

202 FILIGRANES

Avenue des Arts 39
European Quarter ④
+32 (0)2 511 90 15
www.filigranes.be

This vast French-language bookshop has English books in the basement and international newspapers and magazines near the entrance. It's open on Sundays from 10am and has a bright café at the back where you can start the day with a coffee and croissant.

203 LE PETIT FILIGRANES

Parvis Saint-Pierre
Uccle ⑤
+32 (0)2 343 69 01
www.lepetitfiligranes.be

A mini version of Filigranes bookshop on a quiet square near Wolvendael park. It stocks books, daily newspapers and international magazines, and has a coffee bar where you can perch with your newspaper.

204 LE LOUIS D'OR

Rue du Bailli 54
Ixelles ⑤
+32 (0)2 640 64 32
www.planpress.com

This is a well-stocked newsagent just off Avenue Louise where you can find the main British newspapers, along with the German, Dutch and Swiss press.

205 PRESS LINE SABLON

Place du Grand Sablon
Sablon ③
+32 (0)2 503 23 07

Here you can find a good selection of international newspapers on the racks outside the shop, along with a range of specialised magazines inside.

205 PRESS LINE SABLON

The 5 best
STREET MARKETS

206 **JEU DE BALLE**
Place du Jeu de Balle
Marolles ③

Every day, starting at 6am, dealers come to this square to sell boxes of books, dubious oil paintings, art deco lamps, boxes filled with telephones and stacks of ancient LP records. Some dealers have trellis tables. Others lay out their stuff on a carpet. You have no idea what you will find here. A stuffed bear might appear one day, or a beautiful chandelier. The best things are quickly snapped up by professional dealers, so that by midday there is almost nothing left worth buying, unless you are truly interested in a 1962 reel-to-reel tape deck that no longer works.

207 **CHÂTELAIN**
Place du Châtelain
Ixelles ⑤

Each Wednesday, the fashionable Place du Châtelain is the setting for one of the city's most charming street markets. Among the stallholders, you will find a dedicated mushroom seller, a French woman who can tell you exactly the right moment to serve a particular cheese and a pastry chef who once made cakes for Harrods. What

206 JEU DE BALLE

makes this market special is that everyone is relaxed, chatting with one another, lingering in the late afternoon sunshine. It could almost be a village square in rural Provence. After visiting the market, many people head off to one of the wine bars in the neighbourhood or pick up a quick slice of pizza at Mamma Roma.

208 MIDI

Gare du Midi ⑦
Central Brussels

It's cheap. Everyone agrees on that. But the market next to Midi Station is always a bit of a scrum. You end up struggling through the crowd with a huge sack of oranges because, at €4, how could you resist?

209 FLAGEY

Place Flagey
Ixelles ⑤

Every Sunday morning, people living around the Ixelles Ponds make their way to the market on Place Flagey. It has the usual things – vegetable stalls, cheap clothes, a big truck selling chickens roasted on the spot. But it also has plant stalls where locals pick up something to brighten up their small Ixelles back garden and even a champagne bar.

210 BOITSFORT

Place Wiener
Boitsfort

Boitsfort's Sunday market has the feel of a small French town, with vans crammed into the narrow lanes around the art nouveau town hall. Everyone is relaxed as they pick up something for lunch, or a bunch of flowers, or 100 grams of Greek olives.

The 5 best
FLOWER SHOPS

---

211 **DANIEL OST**
Rue Royale 13
Central Brussels ①
+32 (0)2 217 29 17
www.danielost.be

Daniel Ost's ephemeral floral creations have won him many fans in Japan. His flower shop in the Rue Royale lies behind a flamboyant 1896 art nouveau façade created by the architect Paul Hankar. It is the perfect setting for Ost's unique blend of Western and Japanese ideas.

212 **THIERRY BOUTEMY**
Avenue Louise 404
Ixelles ⑤
+32 (0)2 649 39 49

The French florist Thierry Boutemy created the baroque bouquets for Sophia Coppola's film *Marie Antoinette*. His shop is discretely located in a townhouse on Avenue Louise.

213 **BO FLOWER BAR**
Place du Châtelain 49
Ixelles ⑤
+32 (0)2 646 66 96
www.boflowers.be

This friendly shop sells flowers in pots that can last a whole year as well as gorgeous bouquets to take to a friend when you are invited to dinner.

214 HET WITTE GRAS

Rue Plétinckx 7
Saint-Géry ②
+32 (0)2 502 05 29
www.hetwittegras.be

The hip young people who live in apartments around Place Saint-Géry pick up their blooms at this beautiful corner shop. The owner sells tulips in metal buckets, irises in glass vases and sleek white orchids in ceramic pots.

215 VELVET CAFÉ

Chaussée de Charleroi 161
Saint-Gilles ⑥
+32 (0)2 534 07 58
www.velvetine.be

A specialised shop filled with gorgeous orchids from the remotest regions. The knowledgeable owner can advise on the right plants for different rooms in a Brussels house.

The 5 best places for
GRAPHIC ART AND PAPER

216 **PLAIZIER**
Rue des Eperonniers 50
Central Brussels ①
+32 (0)2 513 47 30
www.plaizier.be

This little art shop has been publishing postcards, posters and calendars since 1977. The cards range from whimsical cartoons by Flemish illustrator Ever Meulen to photographs of modern Brussels buildings.

217 **PAPERS**
Rue de Flandre 19
Central Brussels ②
www.papers-gallery.com

This mysterious, fascinating shop, located in an 18th century town house, is dedicated to the art of ancient paper. The owner is a Parisian who collects single sheets of vintage paper, fine notebooks and early fashion drawings.

218 **NATIONAL LIBRARY SHOP**
Mont des Arts
Central Brussels ①
www.krb.be

The little shop in the entrance hall of the national library sells beautiful engravings by Belgian artists like Rops, Khnopff and Evenpoel. Prices are not too high.

219 LE TYPOGRAPHE

Rue Américaine 67
Ixelles ⑤
+32 (0)2 345 16 76

A traditional printing workshop close to Place du Châtelain where they will print your business cards or wedding invitations. The shop sells sublime notebooks and writing paper.

220 MA MAISON DE PAPIER

Galerie de Ruysbroeck
Sablon ③
+32 (0)2 512 22 49
www.mamaisondepapier.be

Here is a vast storehouse of vintage posters on every imaginable theme. The owner, Marie-Laurence Bernard, is an expert on poster design, and pulls open drawers to reveal sublime mementoes, like an old tourist poster for Copenhagen that shows a policeman stopping the traffic to let some ducks cross the road. Prices can be surprisingly high.

216 PLAIZIER

25 BUILDINGS
TO ADMIRE

———

The 5 most striking
ART NOUVEAU HOUSES

---

221 MAISON HANKAR
Rue Defacqz 71
Ixelles ⑤

The Maison Hankar, built by the architect Paul Hankar in 1893, is one of the buildings that launched the art nouveau movement. More than 1,000 art nouveau buildings, from houses to department stores, where built in Brussels between 1893 and 1913, but about half of them have been demolished.

222 MAISON CIAMBERLANI
Rue Defacqz 48
Ixelles ⑤

This beautiful house, recently restored by its owner, was built by Paul Hankar in 1897. It was built for the Symbolist painter Albert Ciamberlani, whose work can be seen in Saint-Gilles town hall.

223 MAISON SAINT-CYR
Square Ambiorix 11
European Quarter ④

A narrow house with a feverishly-ornate façade of iron and glass, built by Gustave Strauven in 1903.

224 MAISON CAUCHIE
Rue des Francs 5
Etterbeek ④
www.cauchie.be

A remarkable art nouveau house built by architect and decorator Paul Cauchie. The architect added the delicate sgraffiti murals on the façade to advertise his skills as a decorator. Open to the public on the first weekend of each month.

225 RUE VANDERSCHRICK

Rue Vanderschrick
Saint-Gilles ⑥

Ernest Blérot designed all the houses on one side of this street in a lively art nouveau style. Each house is decorated differently, with bay windows, wrought iron balconies and carved doors providing visual excitement.

222 MAISON CIAMBERLANI

221 MAISON HANKAR

The 5 best
UNESCO WORLD
HERITAGE SITES

226 GRAND'PLACE

Grand'Place ①
Central Brussels

No one can argue with the decision to add Grand'Place to the UNESCO list of world heritage. Most of the buildings are 17th century guild houses, built soon after much of the square was destroyed by a French bombardment in 1695, but the town hall is an older Gothic building.

227 STOCLET HOUSE

Avenue de Tervuren 279
Woluwe-Saint-Pierre ④

You can admire the front of the house built by the Austrian architect Josef Hoffman in 1905, but you will probably never see inside. It was added to the UNESCO list of world heritage in 2009 as "one of the most accomplished buildings of the Vienna Secession", but few people have been allowed past the front door. Built for the banker and art collector Adolphe Stoclet, it is said to contain works by the Vienna artists Koloman Moser and Gustav Klimt.

228 HOTEL TASSEL
Rue Paul-Emile Janson 6
Ixelles ⑤

In 2000, UNESCO approved an application to add "the four major town houses of Victor Horta" to the world heritage list. The Hôtel Tassel headed the list as the first building ever designed in the art nouveau style. Commissioned by Professor Emile Tassel in 1893, it launched a movement that spread across Europe.

229 HOTEL SOLVAY
Avenue Louise 224
Ixelles ⑤

Victor Horta's Hôtel Solvay was built for one of the country's wealthiest industrialists between 1894 and 1898. The UNESCO report noted that the house was saved from demolition in 1957 when it was bought by the Wittamer-De Camps fashion house. The town house is occasionally open to the public. Otherwise, you can stand on the street and admire Horta's attention to every minor detail including the carved house number.

230 HOTEL VAN EETVELDE
Avenue Palmerston 4
European Quarter ④

The Hôtel Van Eetvelde was built by Horta in 1895-1901 as a family home, but is now owned by the Belgian gas federation. There have been some "unfortunate changes," says UNESCO, but it remains one of Horta's masterpieces.

The 5 finest
ART NOUVEAU BUILDINGS
open to the public

---

231 **HORTA MUSEUM**
Rue Américaine 25
Saint-Gilles ⑥
+32 (0)2 543 04 90
www.hortamuseum.be

Victor Horta's private home and studio in Saint-Gilles commune was turned into a museum in 1961. Horta designed everything from the door handles to the astonishing attic.

232 **OLD ENGLAND**
Montagne de la Cour 2
Central Brussels ①
+32 (0)2 545 01 30
www.mim.be

This flamboyant art nouveau department store was designed by Paul Saintenoy using glass and wrought iron. It is now occupied by the Museum of Musical Instruments.

233 **LA MAISON AUTRIQUE**
Chaussée de Haecht 266
Schaerbeek ⑨
+32 (0)2 215 66 00
www.autrique.be

One of the most inspiring buildings in Brussels, the Maison Autrique was built by Victor Horta in 1893 and restored by the comic book illustrator François Schuiten in 2004. Schuiten imaginatively added details that hint at the lives of the people who once lived here, some of it pure fantasy, like the attic crammed with the imagined collection of the eccentric inventor Axel Wappendorf.

234 **HOTEL HANNON**
Avenue de la Jonction 1
Saint-Gilles ⑥
+32 (0)2 538 42 20
www.contretype.org

This striking art nouveau corner house was built by Jules Brunfaut in 1902 for the engineer Eduard Hannon. The interior includes a wistful smoking room with a large bay window and several fin-de-siècle frescos. Now occupied by the Contretype photography gallery.

235 **COMIC STRIP MUSEUM**
Rue des Sables 20
Central Brussels ①
+32 (0)2 219 19 80
www.cbbd.be

The comic strip museum occupies a former department store built by Victor Horta. The museum has a small exhibition on the ground floor devoted to the many demolished Horta buildings.

234 HOTEL HANNON

The 5 best
ARCADES

---

236 GALERIES SAINT HUBERT

Rue du Marché aux Herbes
Central Brussels ①

The beautiful Galeries Saint Hubert was a sensation when it opened in 1847. It was the world's first shopping arcade, with shops, a theatre, restaurants, cafés and apartments all under one roof. It is still an alluring place where specialised shops sell German cutlery, Italian gloves and Belgian chocolates.

237 GALERIE BORTIER

Rue de la Madeleine
Central Brussels ①

The Galerie Bortier is a romantic 19th century arcade with wood-panelled walls and a glass roof. Never as successful as the Saint-Hubert arcade, it is mainly occupied by antique print shops and secondhand booksellers.

238 PASSAGE DU NORD

Rue Neuve
Central Brussels ①

A 19th century arcade decorated with iron statues of female caryatides. The shops include a cutlery shop and a tiny oyster bar.

240 GALERIE RAVENSTEIN

239 GALERIES AGORA
Rue du Marché aux
Herbes 101
Central Brussels ①

This arcade close to Grand'Place feels like a North African souk. It is crammed with small shops selling leather jackets, cheap jewellery and records.

240 GALERIE RAVENSTEIN
Rue Ravenstein
Central Brussels ①

This impressive modernist arcade was built in the 1950s to link Central Station with the Palais des Beaux Arts. It used to be a gloomy place lined with dark bars, but it now has bookshops, a branch of Exki and an architecture studio.

The 5 most
CURIOUS BUILDINGS

241 **ATOMIUM**
Square de l'Atomium
Heysel
+32 (0)2 475 47 75
www.atomium.be

One of the world's most bizarre structures, the Atomium was designed for Expo 58 to represent an atom magnified several billion times. Following a recent renovation, it shines as brightly as it did in 1958. Best seen at night when the spheres are lit by thousands of tiny lights.

242 **LA BELLONE**
Rue de Flandre 46
Central Brussels ②
+32 (0)2 513 33 33
www.bellone.be

Here is one of the best kept secrets in Brussels. A perfectly preserved 17th century stone house stands on a cobbled courtyard protected from the rain by a modern glass roof. It is truly surreal. The Maison Bellone now houses several cultural organisations and serves as a venue for dance and theatre productions.

243 **GARE DE LA CHAPELLE**
Rue des Ursulines 25
Marolles ③
+32 (0)2 502 57 34
www.recyclart.be

The Gare de la Chapelle is almost a ghost station. All but a few local trains go straight through the station without stopping. It has now been transformed into an alternative art centre called 'Recyclart' where every available wall is covered with graffiti.

244 SAINT GILLES TOWN HALL

Place Van Meenen
Saint-Gilles ⑥

This town hall was designed to resemble a French château and is filled with 19th century art. Go through the entrance to the left of the main staircase and climb the marble staircase to the first floor. After admiring the huge frescos by Ciamberlani, go through the door on the right and walk to the end of the corridor. The last room contains a huge painting of Napoleon in Paris that once formed part of a circular panorama displayed in Paris.

245 PALAIS DE JUSTICE

Place Poelaert
Central Brussels ③

Joseph Poelaert designed the vast law courts in the late 19th century in a strange mixture of architectural styles. The building is an endless warren of staircases, corridors and courtrooms. The government is currently trying to figure out what to do with this crumbling monstrosity, but there is no easy answer.

243 GARE DE LA CHAPELLE

PORTE DE HAL

80 PLACES TO DISCOVER BRUSSELS

The 5 most
UNEXPECTED VIEWS

—————

246 **AROMA COFFEE LOUNGE**
Grand'Place 37
Central Brussels ①
+32 (0)2 513 58 85
www.aromacoffee.be

Grand'Place was voted the most beautiful square in Europe in a recent Dutch survey. But where do you sit to enjoy the view? Some people perch on stone benches, others sit on the first floor of Le Roi d'Espagne. For the best view of all, enter the Aroma coffee house, buy a coffee and take it upstairs. You might get a window table on the first floor. If not, go up one more floor and you come to a small room with seating for about ten people. Almost no one ever comes here, so you can sit at the table next to the window and enjoy a privileged view of Grand'Place.

247 **NATIONAL LIBRARY**
Mont des Arts
Central Brussels ①
www.krb.be

Here is one of the city's most secret places. Take the lift to the 5th floor of the National Library and follow the signs to the cafeteria. You can buy a coffee here and enjoy one of the finest views of the city. Open Monday to Friday 9am to 3.30pm.

248 PARKING 58

Rue de l'Evêque 1
Central Brussels ②

Locals are campaigning to save the car park Parking 58 from demolition. You might wonder why anyone would want to save this run-down relic of Expo 58. The reason is found when you take the dilapidated lift to the top, level 10. Almost no one parks up here, but you get a fascinating view of the old centre of Brussels. The mixture of baroque towers and modern office buildings is hardly beautiful, but it is undoubtedly fascinating. It may all be gone one day. Enjoy it while you can.

249 CROSLY BOWLING

Boulevard de
l'Empereur 36
Central Brussels ③

Crosly Bowling looks more like a petrol station than a bowling alley. It stands uncomfortably next to a stretch of mediaeval city wall. Go inside and climb to the top floor, where you can sit on the terrace with a coffee enjoying an unexpected urban view.

250 CINQUANTENAIRE ARCH

Musée de l'Armée
Parc du Cinquantenaire
European Quarter ④
+32 (0)2 737 78 11
www.klm-mra.be

You can reach the top of the Cinquantenaire arch, built in 1905, by going into the Army Museum and following the sign to 'Arcades'. The lift takes you up to the top of the arch where you get a panoramic view of the European Quarter and the Avenue de Tervuren.

The 5 best places to
UNDERSTAND THE HISTORY OF BRUSSELS

251 HALLES SAINT-GÉRY

Place Saint-Géry 1
Central Brussels ②
+32 (0)2 289 26 60
www.sintgorikshallen.be

The Halles Saint-Géry stand on the site of the marsh where Brussels began. You can find out a little about the history by reading the information panels inside the 1882 former meat hall. The obelisk in the middle was moved here from an abbey outside Brussels.

252 MUSEE DE LA VILLE DE BRUXELLES

Grand'Place
Central Brussels ①
+32 (0)2 279 43 50

The interesting Brussels city museum occupies a 19th century neo-Gothic building on Grand'Place. Here you can see 16th century paintings, photographs of the River Senne before it vanished, and a strange collection of outfits worn by Manneken Pis.

253 COUDENBERG

Place des Palais 7
Central Brussels ①
www.coudenberg.com

The Place Royale stands on the site of a splendid palace that burnt down in 1731. All that remains are the cellars and a stretch of mediaeval street hidden beneath the paving stones. This secret underground complex is reached through a tunnel running from the Bellevue museum (where you buy the entrance ticket).

254 BRUSSELS CITY ARCHIVES

Rue des Tanneurs 65
Marolles ③
+32 (0)2 279 53 20
www.archives.bruxelles.be

No one ever visits the Brussels city archives. They occupy a beautiful old building in the Marolles which was once a fabric store. All the original fittings are preserved, including an iron lift. The museum organises exhibitions on Brussels history, but it unhelpfully closes at weekends.

255 PLACE DES MARTYRS

Off Rue Neuve
Central Brussels ①

A forgotten 18th century square with a romantic monument in the middle in honour of the 466 rebels who died in the 1830 revolution. Several buildings on the square are currently occupied by the Flemish government and one house is owned by a Belgian woman who refuses to restore her façade.

254 BRUSSELS CITY ARCHIVES

The 5 best remains of
THE CITY WALLS

---

256 PORTE DE HAL
Boulevard du Midi 142
Central Brussels ⑥

The Porte de Hal is the only relic to survive from the city's second wall. The rest was torn down in the 19th century to build a ring of tree-lined boulevards (now an urban motorway). The gate has a beautiful spiral staircase leading to the roof.

257 TOUR NOIRE
Rue du Vieux Marché aux Grains
Central Brussels ②

A forgotten relic of the first city wall is enclosed on three sides by a modern hotel. How that happened is a typical Brussels story. The 12th century tower was scheduled for demolition, but in 2000 a local action group persuaded the city to save it. The developers then had to modify their plans to incorporate this rugged symbol of mediaeval defiance.

258 RADISSON BLU HOTEL
Rue du Fossé-aux-Loups 47
Central Brussels ①

A rebuilt stretch of the city's 12th century wall runs through the atrium of the Radisson Hotel. Another stretch can be spotted in the car park to the right of the hotel.

259 **CROSLY BOWLING**
Boulevard de
l'Empereur 36
Central Brussels ③

A 12th century tower with a short stretch of wall can be found next to a bowling alley and petrol station. Two thin strips of blue light set in the pavement mark the former course of the 12th century city wall.

260 **SINT JORIS INSTITUUT**
Rue des Alexiens 16
Central Brussels ①

The longest stretch of the 12th century city wall runs along the back of a school playground. The outside of the wall can be seen from the school courtyard while the inside is visible in Rue du Chêne.

259 **CROSLY BOWLING**

260 **SINT JORIS INSTITUUT**

The 5 most interesting
PLAQUES

---

261 **CHARLOTTE BRONTË**
Rue Baron Horta
Central Brussels ①

Almost no one notices the dusty plaque on the wall of the Bozar cultural centre. It marks the site of the school where Charlotte Brontë and her sister Emily stayed in 1842-43.

262 **RIMBAUD**
Rue des Brasseurs 1
Central Brussels ①

A lace shop occupies the site of the Hôtel à la Ville de Courtrai where the poet Arthur Rimbaud stayed in 1873. The plaque above the entrance notes that Rimbaud was shot by his friend Verlaine in a nearby street.

263 **PUCCINI**
Avenue de la Couronne 1
Ixelles ⑤

A grimy plaque on an apartment building marks the site of the clinic where, in 1924, the Italian composer Giacomo Puccini died. He had travelled to Brussels to receive treatment for throat cancer.

264 **KARL MARX**
Rue Jean d'Ardenne 50
Ixelles ⑤

Karl Marx began working on The Communist Manifesto while living in a house in Ixelles. A plaque put up by the local history society marks the site.

265 **FELIX NUSSBAUM**

Rue Archimède 22
European Quarter ④

The German-Jewish artist Felix Nussbaum and his Polish wife Felka Platek hid from the Nazis for two years in a small attic room at Rue Archimède 22. The couple were eventually deported and killed. A plaque marks the site.

262 **RIMBAUD**

The 5 last traces of
THE RIVER SENNE

---

266 **PLACE SAINT-GÉRY**
Place Saint-Géry 23
Central Brussels ②

The little River Senne meandered through Brussels up until the middle of the 19th century. It was then vaulted over in an attempt to stop the spread of cholera. Almost nothing has survived of the river, but go into a courtyard next to the Halles Saint-Géry and you will find a stretch of water that ends at a blank wall. It's not the river, but shows what it once looked like.

267 **SEWERS MUSEUM**
Porte d'Anderlecht
Boulevard Poincaré
Central Brussels ⑦
+32 (0)2 279 60 13

The River Senne runs through a dark concrete tunnel below the Porte d'Anderlecht. It is now sadly no more than a sewer. You can take a guided tour led by a sewer worker along subterranean walkways dating from the 19th century. You learn a lot, perhaps too much, about rats, floods and peak times for discarded condoms.

268 QUARTIER SAINT JACQUES

Facing Rue du Marché
au Charbon 91
Central Brussels ①

A small but determined action group called les Fous de la Senne, the Senne Idiots, has launched a campaign to bring back the river. The Fous are not totally mad. They know the river can never be restored. So they have settled on bringing back hints of the river, like the thin trickle of water than runs down a gutter next to the Eglise Saint-Jacques.

269 LA GRANDE ECLUSE

La Grande Ecluse
Boulevard Poincaré 77
Anderlecht ⑦
www.grande-ecluse.be

The restaurant La Grande Ecluse occupies a former machine room that operated the locks on the Senne. The small tables are squeezed between some impressive industrial machinery.

270 ANSPACH FOUNTAIN

Quai aux Briques
Central Brussels ②

Walk to the end of the fishmarket to admire the extravagant fountain built to commemorate Jules Anspach, the Brussels mayor who covered over the Senne. It is surrounded by crocodiles spouting water, but most people miss the marble figure of a naked woman who sits uncomfortably in a tunnel. She represents the Senne.

The 5 best
SMALL MUSEUMS

---

271 **WIERTZ MUSEUM**
Rue Vautier 62
Ixelles ⑤
www.fine-arts-museum.be

A French magazine recently listed this as one of the most beautiful museums in the world. And it is. The only problem is that the opening hours are maddening. It's just about impossible to visit at a weekend, or during lunchtime. But persevere and you will find yourself more or less the only visitor in a perfectly-preserved 19th century artist's studio once occupied by the romantic painter Antoine Wiertz. His paintings are vast and gruesome.

272 **CONSTANTIN MEUNIER MUSEUM**
Rue de l'Abbaye 59
Ixelles ⑤
www.fine-arts-museum.be

Ring the bell and wait. Someone will eventually open the door. You may be the only visitor in Constantin Meunier's former home and studio. Yet this is a fascinating place with a huge workshop filled with statues of robust dock workers and reapers, along with sketches of ironworks, paintings of tobacco girls in Seville and boxes of old paintbrushes that belonged to the artist.

273 ERASMUS HOUSE

Rue du Chapitre 31
Anderlecht
+32 (0)2 521 13 83
www.erasmushouse.
museum

Take the metro to Saint-Guidon and look for the church spire. The Erasmus Museum is near the church. The 16th century writer stayed briefly in this mellow brown brick house in the summer of 1521. It is now filled with mementoes of the Dutch scholar, including paintings, cartoons and a reconstructed studio. The little garden at the back is one of the most romantic spots in the city.

274 CHARLIER MUSEUM

Avenue des Arts 16
European Quarter
+32 (0)2 218 53 82
www.charliermuseum.be

Victor Horta designed this house in 1890 for the 19th century sculptor Guillaume Charlier. But don't expect an art nouveau masterpiece. Horta was still a young and rather conventional architect. The museum is a quiet place with an interesting collection of 19th century oil paintings.

275 LIBRARIUM

Mont des Arts
Central Brussels ③
www.krb.be

This little-known museum deep inside the national library displays ancient manuscripts and rare books in mysteriously lit spaces. The highlight is a reconstructed study that once belonged to the Brussels writer Michel de Gelderode, which he filled with bizarre statues and relics. Open free, Monday to Saturday.

The 5 most
SECRET STREETS

---

276 RUE D'ISABELLE
Below Place Royale
Central Brussels ①

The mediaeval Rue d'Isabelle used to run from Place Royale to the Cathedral. It was destroyed in the early 20th century, but one short stretch of cobbled lane survived below Place Royale. It now forms part of the Coundenberg underground museum.

277 CHEMIN DU CRABBEGAT
Off Avenue de Fré
Uccle

You leave the city far behind the moment you turn down this old cobbled lane in Uccle. It passes an old inn called Le Cornet before disappearing between steep wooded banks.

278 RUE SAINTE ANNE
Place du Grand Sablon
Central Brussels ③

An ancient arch next to a hotel on the Sablon leads to a hidden lane that almost no one knows about. It brings you to a little square with an art gallery and several antique shops selling masks and Congolese sculpture.

279 RUE TERARKEN

Below Rue Ravenstein 3
Central Brussels ①

A short stretch of mediaeval cobbled lane runs between the Palais des Beaux-Arts and the 15th century Ravenstein House. At the end of the street, a blue plaque marks the site of the Pensionnat Heger where the British writer Charlotte Brontë spent two years.

280 RUE DE LA CIGOGNE

Off Rue de Flandre
Central Brussels ②

This meandering alley paved with bumpy cobblestones has survived untouched in the city centre. The step gable houses date from the 17th century.

The 5 most beautiful
CEMETERIES

---

281 DIEWEG CEMETERY

Dieweg
Uccle

A beautiful abandoned cemetery with ancient tombstones buried under thick ivy. Hergé, the creator of Tintin, is buried here under a simple stone. The cemetery has been deliberately left untouched to allow wildlife to flourish. Walk to the far end to find a sad forgotten cluster of Jewish graves.

282 LAEKEN CEMETERY

Parvis Notre-Dame
Laeken

This wistful cemetery is filled with the grand tombs of 19th century Belgians. Former mayors and military leaders occupy prime spots on major avenues while artists and musicians repose in the minor lanes. The Atelier Salu next to the entrance cast many of the bronze figures of girls weeping and women mourning.

283 IXELLES CEMETERY

Chaussée de
Boondael 428
Ixelles

With its avenues, roundabouts and enamel street signs, Ixelles Cemetery feels like a small town. The grandest tombs are on the main avenue, while artists and architects are buried in less prestigious locations. Buried here are Victor Horta, Constantin Meunier and Ernest Solvay. Look out, too, for the strange gravestone of Marcel Broodthaers, a surrealist artist.

284 BRUSSELS CEMETERY

Avenue du Cimetière
de Bruxelles
Evere

The city's largest cemetery lies in the eastern suburbs, a 30-minute bus ride from the centre. On broad tree-lined avenues, you find the graves of burgomasters and generals. There are also numerous war graves of soldiers who died in various conflicts and an impressive British monument commemorating those who died in the Battle of Waterloo.

285 ENCLOS DES FUSILLÉES

Rue Colonel Bourg
Schaerbeek

The Enclos des Fusillées lies at the end of a cobbled lane under a huge TV and radio broadcasting tower. This forgotten place is the site of a firing range where the British nurse Edith Cavell was executed in 1915. A total of 342 small concrete crosses commemorate victims executed during the First and Second World War.

The 5 best trips on
PUBLIC TRANSPORT

286 **TRAM 44**

One of the best tram rides in the world, tram 44, starts in a gloomy underground station but soon emerges on Avenue de Tervuren. It then rumbles past the Stoclet House on the right and the tram museum on the left before plunging into the forest. The journey ends some 20 minutes later at a quaint 19th century tram station in Tervuren.

287 **TRAM 94**

The perfect way to see the sights for the price of a tram ticket. Board the tram at Botanique (direction Herrmann Debroux) and watch out for the Brussels Park on the left, Place Royale on the right and the Palais de Justice as the tram swings round to join Avenue Louise. Leave at the Bois de la Cambre for a walk in the park or continue to Boitsfort.

288 **TRAM 23**

An interesting ride that takes you all the way from leafy Uccle to the Atomium, with glimpses along the way of the Josaphat Park and the walled grounds of the royal palace.

289 **BUS 71**

Board the bendy bus 71 at Place de Brouckère for a fascinating (but bumpy) ride that takes you past Central Station, the royal palace, the African Quarter, Place Flagey and the Ixelles Ponds. The eccentric Belgian writer Amélie Nothomb claims bus 71 as one of her main sources of inspiration.

290 **NORTH-SOUTH JUNCTION**

Thousands of trains travel each day through the tunnel that links Gare du Nord and Gare du Midi. You can hop on with a valid Brussels transport ticket for a ride that takes you through the five stations. On the way, you glimpse Place Rogier, rattle through two deserted stations and glimpse a giant spider by the graffiti artist Bonom on a building between Gare de la Chapelle and Gare du Midi.

The 5 best
NEIGHBOURHOODS

291 **PARVIS
DE SAINT GILLES**
Metro: Porte de Hal

An authentic neighbourhood with a lively street market, a church, good corner shops and a sublime derelict cinema called Aegidius. Take a look at the faded art nouveau houses in Rue Vanderschrick and end with a coffee in Brasserie Verschueren or La Maison du Peuple.

292 **SAINT-GÉRY**
Metro: Sainte-Catherine

Place Saint-Géry used to be a quiet abandoned square with a derelict 19th century meat market. The quarter was renovated in the Nineties and is now packed with cool bars and little Asian restaurants.

293 **MATONGÉ**
Metro: Porte de Namur

The Matongé quarter, named after a district of Kinshasa, occupies a few blocks close to the Porte de Namur in Ixelles. This once bourgeois neighbourhood is now dotted with Congolese hairdressers, phone shops and bars that spill onto the streets in the summer.

294 **FLAGEY**

Bus 71 to Flagey

This large square stands on the site of a lake. It is dominated by Flagey, a vibrant arts centre in a former radio broadcasting building. The square has a large Portuguese community, while nearby Rue Malibran is a lively Moroccan street. With its mix of artists, foreigners and older Belgians, Flagey is as multicultural as it gets.

295 **MAROLLES**

Metro: Porte de Hal

The old working class district of Brussels is slowly gentrifying, but it is still an area where life is hard. You see smart antique shops and cool coffee bars on Rue Haute, but also a hospital for the poor and one of Europe's last authentic flea markets.

295 MAROLLES

The 5 best
HIDDEN PARKS

---

296 **PARC D'EGMONT**
Rue aux Laines 1,
Boulevard de Waterloo
31 and 38
Central Brussels ④

Here is one of the loveliest parks in the city, though many people do not even know it exists. The park has a few benches, a statue of Peter Pan and a former orangerie where you can take afternoon tea.

297 **PARC DE FOREST**
Avenue du Mont
Kemmel
Saint-Gilles ⑥

A bit neglected, the Parc de Forest is still a pleasant spot for a Sunday morning walk. It stands on a steeply sloping site surrounded by art nouveau houses with picturesque turrets and gables poking above the trees.

298 **PARC TENBOSCH**
Chaussée de Vleurgat
Square Henri Michaux
Ixelles ⑤

It's all too easy to walk straight past this tiny Ixelles park hidden behind the Indian embassy. But go down the little lane and you will discover a pond with turtles, a playground and a sandpit hidden behind a circular hedge.

299 PARC TOURNAY-SOLVAY

Chaussée de la Hulpe
Watermael-Boitsfort

This is a romantic landscaped park on the forest's edge where the industrialist Ernest Solvay built a country house in 1878. The house is now a charred ruin overlooking a lake, but the rose garden is one of the city's most secret places.

300 PARC FAIDER

Rue Faider 86
Ixelles ⑤

Almost no one knows about this park. It is hidden behind a town house, reached through the coach gate. Locals bring their children, sit with a book, eat a sandwich. It is one of the small pleasures of this city.

296 PARC D'EGMONT

The 5 best
SMALL SQUARES

---

301 PLACE DU JARDIN AUX FLEURS
Tram: Bourse

What makes the perfect Brussels square? It should have at least one café, some metal chairs on the pavement, a fountain in the middle, and a restaurant that has been around for decades. This square has all of that. And there's also a laundromat. Perfect.

302 PLACE DE LA LIBERTÉ
Metro: Madou

This sleepy 19th century square has a few modest cafés along one side and a statue of one of the country's founding fathers in the middle. It's most romantic in the summer when the cafés set out tables under the trees.

303 PLACE DE L'EUROPE
Metro: Gare Centrale

Peter Swinnen, now the Flemish master architect, designed a new square in front of Central Station in 2010. He removed the snarling traffic, added a curved canopy and created a calm pedestrian space to welcome people to the capital of Europe.

304 PLACE SAINT BONIFACE

Metro: Porte de Namur

The local commune recently renovated this lively little square in Ixelles. The stonework on the 19th century Eglise Saint Boniface now gleams like new and Ernest Blérot's lovely art nouveau houses have become a little bit more desirable. The restaurants and cafés put out tables in the summer, leaving a narrow space where cars can just about squeeze through.

305 PLACE DE LONDRES

Metro: Trône

This renovated square on the edge of the Matongé has a few café tables under the trees. It has become a popular spot for young professionals from the European Quarter who find Place du Luxembourg too crowded.

The 5 strangest
URBAN DETAILS

---

306 BERLIN WALL
Place du Luxembourg
Ixelles ⑤

Two weathered sections from the Berlin Wall stand on a square near the European Parliament, while a third section of wall is located in the bushes behind the Parliament. Many young tourists have no idea what these concrete blocks symbolise. Don't they teach history anymore?

307 MAROLLES LIFT
Place Poelaert
Square Brueghel
Marolles ③

Two modern lifts take you in a few seconds from the Marolles to the Palais de Justice. You get fantastic views from the top, especially at night. The lifts are free.

308 RUE VANDENBRANDEN
②

This was an ugly back street until Frédéric Nicolay (see the 5 people who built modern Brussels) decided to give it a facelift. He planted 40 apple trees, brought in some tree trunks to serve as benches, covered a blank wall with wooden pallets and painted a garage door white so that open-air movies could be screened. So simple.

309 STREET SIGNS

Rue des Sables
Central Brussels

All street signs in Brussels are in two languages, French and Dutch. But some streets in central Brussels are also named in the local Brussels dialect, while a cluster of 30 streets near Grand'Place are also named bilingually after comic book characters. So the Rue des Sables (Zandstraat in Dutch) is also the Rue Schtroumpf (Smurfstraat in Dutch). No wonder taxi drivers get lost.

310 BRUEGEL FOUNTAINS

Rue de Rollebeek 2
Central Brussels ③

Not many people notice the little fountains dotted around the old town that are decorated with figures copied from paintings by Pieter Bruegel, including one in the cobbled Rue de Rollebeek, next to a restaurant with the charming name *Et qui va promener le chien?* – And who is going to walk the dog?

309 STREET SIGNS

The 5 best
FLEMISH PLACES

---

311 DE LOKETTEN

Rue de la Croix de Fer
99
Central Brussels ①
+32 (0)2 552 46 11
www.vlaamsparlement.be

Belgians used to visit De Loketten to cash postal orders, but the former post office building is now occupied by the Flemish Parliament. The vast hall has been preserved intact, complete with the original cash desks, and is now used for exhibitions by leading Flemish artists and designers. It also has a café where you can drink Flemish beers, including the Parliament's house brew.

312 KVS

Rue de Laeken 146
Central Brussels ②
+32 (0)2 210 11 00
www.kvs.be

The main Flemish theatre in Brussels occupies an impressive 19th century building in a slightly seedy neighbourhood. The auditorium has been modernised to create a striking performance space, while the bar is one of the grandest in Brussels.

313 KAAITHEATER

Place Sainctelette 20
Central Brussels ⑧
+32 (0)2 201 59 59
www.kaaitheater.be

Some of the most edgy theatre and dance in Europe is staged in a former art deco revue theatre near the canal. Look out for performances by Rosas dance company, Forced Entertainment and the Wooster Group.

314 **MUNTPUNT**
Place de la Monnaie
Central Brussels ①
+32 (0)2 229 18 40
www.muntpunt.be

The Flemish library is a good place to borrow CDs, DVDs and books, or simply to discover the Dutch-speaking culture of Brussels. The architects B-architecten won a competition to redesign the building, which is due to reopen at the end of 2012.

315 **ATELIER BOUWMEESTER**
Rotunda
Galerie Ravenstein
Central Brussels ①

The Flemish master architect, Peter Swinnen, opened a studio in the Galerie Ravenstein in 2012. The space is to be used for architecture exhibitions, discussions and art installations.

315 ATELIER BOUWMEESTER

The 5 most
REMARKABLE PLACES
in the EUROPEAN QUARTER

─────

316 SQUARE DE MEEUS
⑤

The European Quarter is now dominated by concrete office buildings and heavy traffic, but it was originally an elegant 19th century suburb with grand town houses and leafy squares. The little park in the Square de Meeus has kept much of its 19th century character.

317 PARC LEOPOLD
④

This beguiling park with steep slopes and a lakeside walk was once a 16th century country estate. It briefly became a 19th century zoo before being reincarnated as an early 20th century science park. It is now a convenient shortcut between the European Parliament and the Berlaymont building, as well as a quiet place to soak up the sun.

318 SQUARE AMBIORIX
④

A romantic 19th century square on the edge of the European Quarter where elderly Turkish men play card games and Eurocrats eat their sandwiches.

319 RESIDENCE PALACE
Rue de la Loi 155
European Quarter ④

This luxury apartment block built in the 1920s is now a press centre occupied by international journalists and TV stations. It has a striking Moorish entrance hall and a smart café-restaurant. The Council of the European Union is due to move into one wing of the building in 2013. Until then the area around the building is a massive construction site.

320 BERLAYMONT PANELS
Rond Point Schuman
European Quarter ④

You may want to know how the European Commission ended up in the Berlaymont building. This fascinating story is told in a series of information panels attached to glass screens on the south side of the building.

The 5 most
DECADENT PLACES

---

321 HOTEL LE BERGER

Rue du Berger 24
Ixelles ⑤
+32 (0)2 510 83 40
www.lebergerhotel.be

Le Berger was once a discreet rendezvous hotel where couples could rent a small room for three hours of passion. Built in 1933, it had two lifts so that guests never saw one another. The hotel closed in 2009 and looked set for demolition, but was saved by the group behind the fashionable The White Hotel. It has now been tastefully restored to its original slightly risqué art deco style.

322 LES PASSIONS HUMAINES

Parc du Cinquantenaire
European Quarter ④

This little Greek temple in a shady corner of the Parc du Cinquantenaire was designed by Victor Horta to hold a large sculpture by Jef Lambeau titled 'The Human Passions'. This work so shocked the people of Brussels that it had to be locked away. Occasional guided tours are organised by the Musée du Cinquantenaire.

323 LADY PANAME

Rue des Aléxiens 5
Central Brussels ③
+32 (0)2 514 30 35
www.ladypaname.com

A little shop in the Saint-Jacques district, decorated in a cheeky boudoir style. It sells sexy lingerie, erotic novels and tasteful accessories.

324 EVA LUNA

Rue du Bailly 41
Ixelles ⑤
+32 (0)2 647 46 45
www.evaluna.be

A flight of marble steps leads to this seductive little sex shop. The interior is divided into eight themed sections titled so trendy, so nude, so tasty, so romantic, so glamorous, so addict, so cheeky and so man. So take your pick.

325 GALERIE LIBERTINE

Rue Ernest Allard 22
Sablon ③
+32 (0)475 83 31 67
www.galerielibertine.com

This tasteful little gallery of erotic art is located in the heart of the antiques district. The collection includes old engravings, 19th century photographs and erotic curiosities.

323 LADY PANAME

WIELS

40 PLACES TO ENJOY CULTURE

The 5 most inspiring
CULTURAL CENTRES

———

326 **PASSA PORTA**
Rue Dansaert 46
Central Brussels ②
+32 (0)2 502 94 60
www.passaporta.be

A narrow passage off fashionable Rue Dansaert leads to the international literature centre Passa Porta. Its bookshop has an inspiring selection of world literature, including English fiction in the back room. International writers regularly pass this way to give readings or reside in a luxurious writer's flat.

327 **INSTITUTO ITALIANO DI CULTURA**
Rue de Livourne 38
Ixelles ⑤
+32 (0)2 533 27 20
www.iicbruxelles.esteri.it

Try to forget that it was founded by Mussolini and simply enjoy the old Italian movies, the debates in Italian and the language courses.

328 **CASA DE ASTURIAS**
Rue Saint Laurent 36
Central Brussels ①

The Spanish region of Asturias did Brussels a big favour by renovating the abandoned Le Peuple newspaper building. The Spanish architects preserved the modernist architecture but added subtle new touches. The centre has an excellent restaurant and an exhibition space.

329 DAARKOM

**Rue du Fossé aux Loups
18
Central Brussels** ①
+32 (0)2 227 64 10
www.daarkom.be

The old La Gaîté variety theatre has been converted into a Flemish-Moroccan cultural centre using wood and tiles imported from Morocco. The centre organises film screenings, debates and exhibitions. It also has an attractive Moroccan coffee house overlooking Place de la Monnaie.

330 DE BUREN

**Rue Leopold 6
Central Brussels** ①
+32 (0)2 212 19 30
www.deburen.eu

Based in a 19th century building behind La Monnaie, De Buren is a cultural organisation jointly run by the Dutch and Flemish governments. It organises lively debates, photo exhibitions and concerts, mainly in Dutch but sometimes in English.

326 PASSA PORTA

The 5 best
ART GALLERIES

---

331 **WIELS**
   Avenue Van Volxem 354
   Forest
   +32 (0)2 340 00 53
   www.wiels.org

This modern art centre is located in the Wielemans-Ceuppens brewery, built in the concrete modernist style of the 1930s. It hosts exhibitions by edgy contemporary artists and has a smart café located in the former brewing hall.

332 **L'ISELP**
   Boulevard de Waterloo 31
   Ixelles ⑤
   +32 (0)2 504 80 70
   www.iselp.be

This art institute organises small exhibitions by contemporary artists in the former stables of the Egmont Palace. The two-floor building also has a smart restaurant and art bookshop.

333 **JAN MOT**
   Rue Dansaert 190
   Central Brussels ②
   www.janmot.com

This tiny gallery at the low-rent end of Rue Dansaert comes up with inspiring exhibitions by conceptual artists. Jan Mot also produces a lively newspaper to publicise the gallery and its artists.

334 ARGOS

Rue du Chantier 13
Central Brussels ②
+32 (0)2 229 00 03
www.argosarts.org

International video art is screened in a rugged concrete industrial space near the canal zone. The building is divided into a range of interesting spaces including an intimate screening room called the 'Black Box'.

335 XAVIER HUFKENS

Rue Saint Georges 6
Ixelles ⑤
+32 (0)2 639 67 30
www.xavierhufkens.com

Xavier Hufkens exhibits international artists in an Ixelles town house which was converted into a gallery by the Ghent architects Robbrecht & Daem. He brings well-known names like Antony Gormley to Brussels, but also gives generous amounts of space to emerging artists.

331 WIELS

The 5 best
STATUES

336 **PATRIA**
Place des Martyrs
Central Brussels ①

A romantic monument decorated with four weeping women stands in the middle of the forgotten Place des Martyrs. Look more closely and you will see four plaques decorated with scenes from the 1830 Belgian Revolution.

337 **CHARLES BULS**
Place de l'Agora
Rue Marché aux Herbes
Central Brussels ①

A fountain near Grand'Place commemorates the 19th century mayor who saved many old buildings from demolition. Buls sits on a stone bench with his dog at his feet.

338 **BIRTH OF THE NATION**
Opposite Square
Marie-Louise 79
European Quarter ④

A wistful, dreamy statue in a corner of the Square Marie-Louise recalls the Belgian revolution of 1830. Titled 'Birth of the nation', it shows a young couple gazing adoringly at their newborn son. It was carved by the Belgian sculptor Marius Vos, who later emigrated to the United States.

339 **WILLIAM OF ORANGE**
   Place du Petit Sablon
   Central Brussels ③

A statue of William of Orange stands in a green niche in the poetic Petit Sablon park. William of Orange lived for many years in a palace in Brussels, before fleeing north to lead the Dutch revolt against Philip II of Spain.

340 **THE SOLDIER PIGEON**
   Quai aux Bois-à-Brûler
   Central Brussels ②

A statue at the end of the fishmarket commemorates the carrier pigeons that died during World War One. A strange, touching idea.

The 5 best
PAINTINGS IN THE
MUSEUM OF FINE ARTS

---

341 PORTRAIT OF ANTOINE OF BURGUNDY

Van der Weyden's portrait shows a proud artistocrat of the Burgundian court dressed in black with a red cap providing the only colour. Van der Weyden focuses all his attention on the proud, slightly cruel face.

342 THE FALL OF ICARUS

Peter Bruegel the Elder's landscape with the Fall of Icarus is a strange work in which Icarus has already fallen from the sky and vanished below the waves, with just one foot still visible. W.H. Auden wrote a poem about the painting in December 1938, in which he noted, "About suffering they were never wrong, the Old Masters."

343 THE DEATH OF MARAT

One of the great paintings of the French Revolution, Jean-Louis David's 1793 'Death of Marat' is hidden in a basement room. The artist (who lived in exile in Brussels) painted Marat, a revolutionary newspaper editor, soon after he was murdered in his bath by Charlotte Corday.

344 PORTRAIT OF MARGUERITE KHNOPFF

Fernand Khnopff's 1887 portrait of his sister Marguerite represents the cool symbolist style of fin-de-siècle Belgium. She appears chaste and remote, almost a statue.

345 LA VOIX PUBLIQUE

Paul Delvaux's La Voix Publique of 1948 is a strange nocturnal surrealist work showing a naked woman in an antiquated Brussels interior. She is surrounded by three women wearing black dresses while an old Brussels tram approaches. Deeply mysterious.

The 5 best

ART INSTALLATIONS

---

346 **THE WHIRLING EAR**
Mont des Arts
Central Brussels ③

Alexander Calder's mobile sculpture 'The Whirling Ear' originally stood in front of the American pavilion at Expo 58. It then disappeared for several decades, but in 2000 it was dusted down and installed in the middle of a fountain near the Fine Arts Museum.

347 **CEMENT TRUCK**
Quai au Foin
Central Brussels ②

Wim Delvoye's lifesize Gothic cement mixer stands on a quiet square behind the Flemish theatre. It took a lot of persuading before local residents agreed to have this jagged steel artwork in their neighbourhood.

348 **BLUE ON YELLOW**
Place de la Justice
Central Brussels ③
Metro: Gare Centrale

Daniel Buren has brought life to a grey city square with an urban forest of 89 flagpoles flying distinctive blue and yellow flags.

349 THE SEQUENCE

Chaussée de Louvain 86
Central Brussels
Metro: Madou
www.thesequence.be

The Flemish artist Arne Quinze has spanned a Brussels street with an enormous canopy constructed from red wooden slats. The structure, completed in 2008, links the Flemish Parliament with a building occupied by Flemish MPs. The structure has a life span of five years, after which the wood will be recycled.

350 PISSING DOG

Rue des Chatreux
Central Brussels ②

Tom Frantzen's 1999 statue of a dog pissing in the street serves as the perfect symbol of this chaotic but charming city. Frantzen also created a statue of a policeman tripped up by a boy hiding in a manhole.

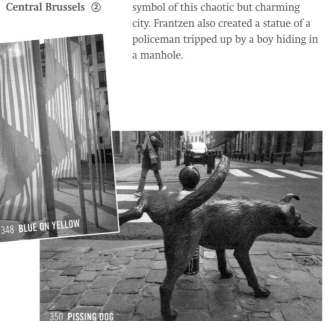

348 BLUE ON YELLOW

350 PISSING DOG

The 5 best places to see
ART IN THE METRO

---

351 ALBERT

The French artist Jephan de Villiers has turned Albert station into an imaginary archaeological museum containing relics from the invented lost city of Arbonie. A massive wooden cart transporting a giant rock stands in a glass case while an underground pit contains several hundred oval objects covered in mysterious writing.

352 COMTE DE FLANDRE

The 16 eerie human figures suspended above the tracks at Compte de Flandre station, titled '16 x Icarus', were made by the Antwerp artist Paul van Hoeydonck in 1981. Ten years earlier, Van Hoeydonck's tiny aluminium figure 'Fallen Astronaut' was laid on the surface of the moon by the Apollo 15 crew. It remains the only work of art on the moon.

353 MAELBEEK

Maelbeek station, in the heart of the European Quarter, is decorated with strange sad faces painted on the tiled walls by the Belgian artist Benoît.

354 PORTE DE HAL

Old Brussels trams poke out of the walls and imaginary cities rise above the station platforms at Porte de Hal station. The Brussels artist François Schuiten created this strange utopian vision in 1993, drawing on his cult comic book *Brüsel*.

355 SIMONIS

The Flemish artist Berlinde De Bruyckere, known for eerie sculptures of human corpses, opted for a less edgy aesthetic in her commission for the busy Simonis (Léopold II) station. She decorated the walls with large carpets made from cement tiles to create a comforting environment.

INFO
www.stib.be

The Brussels transport authority STIB has published a book on art in the metro. It also has information on the art and artists on its website.

354 PORTE DE HAL

The 5 best places to find
STREET ART

356 **LISE BRACHET**
Rue des Chandeliers
Marolles ③

A steep and narrow lane in the Marolles dating from the 12th century has recently been decorated with some imaginative graffiti art. At the top end, the painter Lise Brachet has created a witty series of scenes from the history of Brussels, working with local children.

357 **BONOM**
Chaussée de Wavre 268
Ixelles ⑤
www.bonom.be

The street artist Bonom paints mysterious animal skeletons in unexpected locations across the city. Some disappear within hours, but others have survived. His most impressive work involves several dinosaur skeletons painted on the steps leading up to the Institute of Natural Science.

358 **JEF AEROSOL**
Rue du Chêne 7
Central Brussels ①

The French street artist Jef Aérosol sprayed stencil graffiti portraits of famous rock singers such as John Lennon and Bob Dylan on the grey façade of a downtown record shop. He has also sprayed stencils of a crouching boy in various locations, including Rue des Chartreux.

359 ROA
Rue Chaufferette 25
Central Brussels ①

The secretive Ghent street artist ROA has painted a series of four sleeping wild boar in a narrow lane that almost no one walks down. ROA is well-known in New York and Paris for his animal graffiti, yet this work (signed at the bottom right) attracts little attention.

360 DE WAND MURAL
De Wand tram stop
Trams 4, 19, 23

You glimpse it when you take the tram to the Atomium, but you need to get out at De Wand stop to really appreciate the longest graffiti wall in Europe. Some 30 street artists were commissioned by Brussels Region to decorate an entire wall of this tram station. Titled 'The Walk', it took nine days and 6,000 spray cans to cover 4,500 square metres of bare concrete.

357 BONOM

The 5 best places to discover
RENÉ MAGRITTE

361 **MAGRITTE MUSEUM**
Rue de la Régence 3
Central Brussels ①
+32 (0)2 508 32 11
www.musee-magritte-museum.be

The Magritte Museum opened in 2009 in an impressive neoclassical building on Place Royale. Many of the paintings were bequeathed by Georgette Magritte when she died. So they are not the famous works that Magritte sold to collectors. But it's still a fascinating collection that includes photographs, amateur film footage and surrealist ephemera.

362 **RENÉ MAGRITTE MUSEUM**
Rue Esseghem 35
Jette
+32 (0)2 428 26 26
www.magrittemuseum.be

This is not the Magritte Museum. This is the house in Jette where René and Georgette lived from 1930 to 1957. The great Belgian surrealist created some of the most startling images in modern art in the kitchen of this modest home. It was bought by two art enthusiasts and restored to its original state.

363 **LE GREENWICH**
Rue des Chartreux 7
Central Brussels ②
+32 (0)2 511 41 67

Magritte liked this old creaky bar where local men gather to play chess. The café closed in 2011 to allow the architects Robbrecht & Daem to renovate the belle époque interior. Some worry that its charm will be lost.

364 LA FLEUR EN PAPIER DORÉ

Rue des Alexiens 55
Central Brussels ①
+32 (0)2 511 16 59

Magritte is rumoured to have sold his first painting to one of the regulars in this ancient bohemian café. The three tiny rooms are filled with old furniture, murky paintings and cryptic writings. You won't find anything by Magritte, but go through to the back room to admire the enlarged photograph showing Magritte along with other regulars standing outside the café.

365 SCHAERBEEK CEMETERY

Avenue Jules Bordet
Schaerbeek

Magritte died in 1967 while living at the Rue des Mimosas in Schaerbeek. He was buried in Schaerbeek Cemetery under a plain stone slab, located in plot 16, row 2. His fans sometimes leave curious objects on the grave.

361 **MARGRITTE MUSEUM**

INSTITUTE OF NATURAL SCIENCES

20 THINGS TO DO WITH CHILDREN

The 5 best places to take
SMALL CHILDREN

---

366 INSTITUTE OF NATURAL SCIENCES

Rue Vautier 29
Ixelles ⑤
+32 (0)2 627 42 38
www.naturalsciences.be

Here is the perfect place to take kids on a rainy day. The main attraction is a spectacular gallery displaying more than 30 dinosaur skeletons found in a Belgian coal mine. Other sections cover the Polar regions and ecology.

367 SCIENTASTIC

Bourse underground station
Boulevard Anspach
Central Brussels ②
+32 (0)2 732 13 36
www.scientastic.com

This low-budget private museum is located in an underground station. It sounds grim, but kids have a great time here trying out fun experiments.

368 TURTLEWINGS

Avenue Huart Hamoir 54
Schaerbeek ⑨
+32 (0)2 888 69 19
www.turtlewings.be

This excellent creative studio set up by an American designer lets kids explore their artistic sides. The programme includes children's summer camps, urban exploration trails and even play sessions for adults.

369 C.RAMIC ART CAFÉ

Rue Lesbroussart 112
Ixelles ⑤
+32 (0)2 648 48 72
www.cramic.be

A friendly workshop filled with parents and noisy kids where everyone sits around big wooden benches decorating ceramic cups and bowls. Perfect for a birthday party or a rainy day.

370 MUSÉE DU JOUET

Rue de l'Association 24
Botanique ⑨
+32 (0)2 219 61 68
www.museedujouet.be

This toy museum is located in a rambling Brussels town house. It is run by a man called André who cannot say no. People present him with old train sets, tin cars, sad dolls and hundreds of teddy bears. André does his best to sort it all out, but it's an impossible task and boxes lie unopened by the door, while dolls lie on tables waiting to be repaired. It is utterly chaotic, yet strangely charming.

366 INSTITUTE OF NATURAL SCIENCES

The 5 best
ICE CREAM SHOPS

371 LE FRAMBOISIER DORÉ

Rue du Bailli 35
Ixelles ⑤
+32 (0)2 647 51 44

You can sit in a long upstairs room with a view of the garden or the little green room at the back. Or you can just pick up a cone from the window on the street. The ice creams are handmade without using preservatives. They come in dozens of strange flavours including lavender, *speculoos* and a sublime *caramel au beurre sale* (caramel with salted butter).

372 ZIZI

Rue de la Mutualité 57A
Uccle
www.glacierzizi.be

This popular ice cream shop was opened in 1948 by an Italian called Izzi Gabrielle who started out in Brussels selling ice cream from a cart. The local kids called him Zizi (a slang word for penis). So mothers living in this very smart neighbourhood buy their children a cone from a shop with a very rude name.

373 COMUS & GASTEREA

Quai aux Briques 86
Central Brussels ②

The owner of this ice cream parlour is passionate about his product and creates sublime flavours using natural ingredients. Opening hours are erratic and the queues can be long.

374 IL GELATO

Rue Vanderkindere 168
Uccle
www.ilgelato.be
Bois de la Cambre
summer cabin

When Maurizio Boccia arrived from Italy in 1990 to open an ice cream shop in Uccle, just a few hundred metres from Zizi, it looked like an ice cream war might break out in this quiet Brussels suburb. Il Gelato is a bit more glamorous than Zizi. Its servers are more beautiful. Its advertising campaigns are smarter. 'Our customers are the most beautiful in the world', they claim.

375 CAPOUE

Avenue des Celtes 36
Etterbeek
www.capoue.com

Capoue is devoted to making traditional ice cream with an authentic rough texture. As well as vanilla and chocolate, they like to develop original flavours like champagne or mojito. Now in eight locations across Brussels.

373 COMUS & GASTEREA

The 5 best
COMIC BOOK MURALS

---

376 **RIK HOCHET**
Rue de Bon-Secours
Central Brussels ①

Twenty years ago, a group of fresco artists launched a project to paint scenes from Brussels comic books on blank side walls. They have now completed 37 works in central Brussels. One of the oldest, painted in 1992, shows the cartoon hero Ric Hochet, who appears to be hanging from a real roof gutter. After two decades, the mural now needs some retouching.

377 **XIII**
Rue Philippe
de Champagne 29-31
Central Brussels ①

This striking New York street scene from William Vance's comic series XIII was painted on the side wall of a house in 2010.

378 **NERO**
Place Saint-Géry
Central Brussels ②

Several characters from Marc Sleen's 'The Adventures of Nero & Co' appear in a 1995 mural on a side wall near the Marché Saint-Géry. Marc Sleen has his own museum in Brussels.

379 LE PASSAGE
Rue Marché au Charbon
Central Brussels ①

The comic book illustrator François Schuiten created this trompe l'oeil mural representing an imaginary city. Schuiten also designed the Porte de Hal metro station and helped to restore Horta's Maison Autrique.

380 GASTON LAGAFFE
Rue de l'Ecuyer 9
Central Brussels ①

Look up and you will see Gaston Lagaffe leaning out of a window. Created by Franquin, Lagaffe was a city kid who liked to devise complicated schemes to avoid parking meter charges. On the day this mural was unveiled, the city suspended parking meter charges for 24 hours.

The 5 best places to go on a
TINTIN TOUR

---

381 GARE DU MIDI
Gare du Midi
Horta entrance
Central Brussels ⑦

Tintin hangs onto a steam train in a huge fresco in the Gare du Midi entrance hall. The image comes from the pages of *Tintin in America*, published in 1932.

382 LE LOMBARD
Place Bara
Anderlecht ⑦

A huge revolving sign on the roof of an office building near Gare du Midi shows Tintin and his dog Snowy. The sign was put there by the Lombard publishing company, which publishes the Tintin books, when it moved here in 1958.

383 GARE DU LUXEMBOURG
Place du Luxembourg
Ixelles ⑤

A mural based on an early Hergé cartoon was unveiled in 2009 at the entrance to the Gare du Luxembourg, near the European Parliament. Originally advertising a department store, the drawing is crowded with characters from Hergé's comics.

384 RUE DE L'ETUVE
Rue de l'Etuve 37
Central Brussels ①

A comic book mural on a wall in the busy Rue de l'Etuve shows Tintin running down a fire escape pursued by Captain Haddock. The scene is taken from *The Calculus Affair*.

385 STOCKEL METRO STATION

Woluwé-Saint-Pierre

Blistering barnacles! You arrive at Stockel metro station to see Captain Haddock peering at you through the carriage window. What could be more unsettling? Hergé made the sketches for Stockel station just before his death in 1983. The murals incorporate 140 different characters taken from 22 Tintin comic albums.

381 **GARE DU MIDI**

VINTAGE

20 PLACES
TO SLEEP

The 5 most
LUXURIOUS HOTELS

---

386 DOMINICAN

Rue Léopold 9
Central Brussels ①
+32 (0)2 203 08 08
www.thedominican.be

Located in a former mediaeval monastery, the Dominican was once home to the French artist Jacques-Louis David. Now a sophisticated hotel with an interior designed by the Amsterdam firm FG Stijl, it strikes a calm note in the city centre with its airy cloister, rich fabrics and countless orchids.

387 AMIGO

Rue de l'Amigo
Central Brussels ①
+32 (0)2 547 47 47
www.hotelamigo.com

Built for the Brussels Expo in 1958, the Amigo Hotel looks much older. It is a comfortable, elegant hotel in a prime location off Grand'Place, making it a favourite with Europe's national leaders when they are in town for a summit. The presidential suite has a terrace with a spectacular view of the Gothic town hall.

388 STANHOPE

Rue du Commerce 9
European Quarter ⑤
+32 (0)2 506 91 11
www.stanhope.be

The Stanhope is a refuge of traditional British style amid the concrete horrors of the European Quarter. Occupying three town houses and a modern addition, it is a rambling place where Europe's bureaucrats can retreat after work. The lobby is a cool marble space that was once occupied by a smart pharmacy while the courtyard is a delightfully secluded spot shaded by an old magnolia.

389 LE DIXSEPTIEME

Rue de la Madeleine 25
Central Brussels ①
+32 (0)2 517 17 17
www.ledixseptieme.be

This beautiful, rambling 17th century mansion close to Grand'Place once belonged to the Spanish ambassador. It is now a stylish hotel with large, luxurious rooms.

390 LE PLAZA

Boulevard Adolphe
Max 118
Central Brussels ①
+32 (0)2 278 01 00
www.leplaza-brussels.be

This grand hotel with marble floors and chandeliers was built in 1930 in the style of the Georges V in Paris. It closed down in the Seventies but reopened in 1995 after a costly renovation. It has the grandest lobby in town, along with spacious bedrooms and a curious Moorish theatre. The neighbourhood sadly still has a few old porn cinemas that refuse to budge.

The 5 most
STYLISH B&B'S

391 SWEET BRUSSELS
Avenue de Stalingrad 78
Central Brussels ①
+32 (0)486 25 91 37
www.sweetbrussels.be

A gorgeous 19th century town house located on a tree-lined avenue in the heart of the city. The bedrooms have high ceilings, big windows and old-fashioned bathtubs. And the owner is very sweet.

392 URBAN ROOMS
Rue Alsace Lorraine 10
Ixelles ⑤
+32 (0)471 951 535
www.urbanrooms.be

A friendly couple, both architects, run this hip B&B in a fashionable neighbour-hood close to the EU institutions. The three bedrooms are light and modern, while the terrace at the back is a good place to soak up the sun.

393 COUP DE COEUR
Place de la Vieille Halle
aux Blés 43
Central Brussels ①
+32 (0)474 03 24 70
www.lecoupdecoeur.be

This charming B&B is located in a narrow old house in the town centre. You eat breakfast in a white tiled ground floor room that was once a butcher's shop, while the three bedrooms are up steep wooden stairs. The rooms are vast and achingly romantic.

394 DOWNTOWN BXL

Rue du Marché
au Charbon 118
Central Brussels ①
+32 (0)475 29 07 21
www.downtownbxl.com

This 18th century town house has been converted into a beautiful guesthouse with three spacious bedrooms and a breakfast room furnished with a long communal table. Located on a street crammed with bars and restaurants, this is the perfect location for a lively urban weekend. We would love to spend a night in the romantic duplex in the attic.

395 MAISON NOBLE

Rue Marcq 10
Central Brussels ②
+32 (0)2 219 23 39
www.maison-noble.eu

This 19th century town house, close to the Beguinage, opened in 2007 as the city's first luxury gay guesthouse. It has fine period features like stained glass windows, along with three bright bedrooms, a piano room and a steam room in the basement.

391 SWEET BRUSSELS

The 5 best
SMALL HOTELS

396 MANOS PREMIER

Chaussée de Charleroi
100
Saint-Gilles ⑤
+32 (0)2 537 96 82
www.manospremier.com

This family-owned hotel occupies an old town house near Avenue Louise. It is a charming place that feels like a Belgian family home, with a beautiful conservatory where breakfast is served and an Oriental spa. But tram 92 runs past the hotel so the front rooms are noisy.

397 WELCOME

Quai au Bois-à-Brûler 2
Central Brussels ②
+32 (0)2 219 95 46
www.hotelwelcome.com

This small hotel occupies an old building overlooking the fish market. Each of the 17 rooms is decorated in the style of an exotic destination. So you can stay in a room inspired by Morocco or ask for the dramatic red and black Tibet room.

398 NOGA

Rue du Béguinage 38
Central Brussels ②
+32 (0)2 218 67 63
www.nogahotel.com

Here is a friendly family-run hotel in a quiet street close to the fishmarket. The interior is crammed with odd antiques like in an old Belgian home, while the sitting room welcomes guests with a stack of board games.

399 **REMBRANDT**

Rue de la Concorde 42
Ixelles ⑤
+32 (0)2 512 71 39
www.hotelrembrandt.be

This friendly hotel has a certain period charm. The hall is decorated with solid armchairs and little ornaments. The rooms feel like grandmother has had a hand in the decor. It's in a quiet street near Avenue Louise.

400 **LES TOURELLES**

Avenue Winston
Churchill 135
Uccle ⑤
+32 (0)2 344 95 73
www.lestourelles.be

This old-fashioned hotel occupies a former boarding school for girls on a tree-lined avenue in the suburbs. Drenched in wisteria, it's a charming, romantic place. But only if you like creaking floorboards and old radiators. Worth asking if room 7 is available.

397 WELCOME

The 5 coolest
DESIGN HOTELS

---

401 PANTONE

Place Loix 1
Saint-Gilles ⑥
+32 (0)2 541 48 98
www.pantonehotel.com

The Belgian designers Michel Penneman and Oliver Hannaert have transformed a dull 1970s building into a fashionista hideaway. The design is based on the Pantone system of colour classification, so there are bright splashes everywhere. You can even lounge on a bean bag on the roof terrace sipping a cocktail based on Pantone colour 12-0435.

402 VINTAGE

Rue Dejoncker 45
Saint-Gilles ⑥
+32 (0)2 533 99 80
www.vintagehotel.be

The designer Michel Penneman has done it again, turning a former old people's home near Avenue Louise into a nostalgic hotel filled with quirky design objects from the 1950s and 1960s. You can't help but like the Charles and Ray Eames sofa, the psychedelic wallpaper and the friendly staff. The wine bar with its courtyard terrace adds to the easy charm.

402 **VINTAGE**

403 BLOOM!

Rue Royale 250
Central Brussels ⑨
+32 (0)2 220 66 11
www.hotelbloom.com

In 2008 this standard concrete chain hotel was transformed into a quirky design bolthole aimed precisely at style geeks. Each of the 287 rooms has a fresco painted on the wall behind the bed by a bright young artist straight out of art school. And the website has a sophisticated online booking form that allows you to pick the room you want depending on the artist's nationality, style or the school where they studied.

404 ALOFT

Place Jean Ray
European Quarter ④
+32 (0)2 800 08 88
www.aloftbrussels.com

This striking modern hotel is a beacon of funky cool in the sterile European Quarter. The style is industrial chic and the spacious bar with billiard table is a fun spot to relax. Some may find it just a bit too hip.

405 PACIFIC

Rue Antoine Dansaert 57
Central Brussels ②
+32 (0)2 213 00 80
www.hotelpacific.com

This cute little design hotel in the heart of the fashion district has 12 unique rooms including a gorgeous duplex. The interior design is the work of the brilliant local designer Mia Zia. One of the best small hotels in Brussels.

403 **BLOOM!**

NOVA

45 ACTIVITIES
FOR WEEKENDS

The 5 best
FOREST WALKS

---

406 BOIS DE LA CAMBRE
Main entrance at end
of Avenue Louise

Here is the place to walk on a Sunday.
Landscaped in a 19th century romantic
style, it features artificial crags, a lake
with an island and several restaurants.
Take tram 94 to the Legrand stop and set
off down one of several forest paths to
reach the lake. A mechanical ferry plies
across the water to the Chalet Robinson
restaurant.

407 DRÈVE DU COMTE

A simple tram ride is all it takes to reach
the magnificent beech forest on the
southern edge of Brussels. Take tram 94
to the Coccinelles stop and walk down
the cobbled lane to reach the Etangs des
Enfants Noyées. From here, you can follow several meandering trails that lead
into wild forest.

408 ABBAYE DU ROUGE-CLOÎTRE

Begin at Herrmann-Debroux metro station

Some of the best forest walks begin near the Abbaye du Rouge-Cloître in the Auderghem commune. For a simple one-hour walk, follow the paths named Sluipdelleweg, Verbrandedreef and Vijversweg. A simple café called 'La vita è bella' occupies one of the abbey buildings.

409 TERVUREN WOODS

Tram 44 to Tervuren

The woods to the east of Tervuren were planned under the Austrians in the 18th century. One of the best woodland walks follows the Wilde Zwijnenweg to reach a spot called Zevenster, where trails lead in every direction.

410 ARBORETUM

Walks begin in Jezus-Eik

Head through the woods behind the village of Jezus-Eik and you will eventually come to an area planted with exotic redwoods and monkey puzzle trees. You have reached the arboretum planted during the reign of Leopold II. A car is probably needed to get out here.

INFO

The IGN map of the Forêt de Soignes marks all the trails through the forest.

The 5 best places for
URBAN WALKS

---

411 IXELLES PONDS

Join local families and joggers on a walk around the Ixelles Ponds, beginning at Place Flagey and following the dusty footpaths as far as the Abbaye de la Cambre.

412 EUROPEAN QUARTER

Walk from the Place du Luxembourg through the European Parliament to reach the Parc Leopold. Then follow the meandering paths until you arrive at the main entrance. Cross the Place Jean Ray and climb the hill to Rond Point Schuman to look at the Berlaymont and Justus Lipsius buildings. Eat lunch on Place Jourdan.

413 ART NOUVEAU

Meander down Avenue Louise and its side streets to look at the art nouveau houses built in this neignbourhood from 1893 to 1910. Some of the most striking houses are in the streets between Avenue Louise and the Ixelles ponds.

414 **FASHION**

To find out the latest trends in Belgian fashion, start at the Bourse and walk down Rue Dansaert until you reach the canal, then explore the more funky shops on the Rue des Chartreux.

415 **ANTIQUES**

Begin at the flea market on Place du Jeu de Balle and walk along the Rue Blaes. At the Place de la Chapelle, turn right up the hill to reach the Place du Grand Sablon. The more upmarket antique dealers have their shops on side streets like Rue des Minimes.

The 5 best places to
GET FIT

---

416 ASPRIA ARTS-LOI
Rue de l'Industrie 26
European Quarter ④
+32 (0)2 508 08 00
www.aspria.be

This is one of the best gyms in town. It's also one of the most expensive. But it does have a large swimming pool, a stylish restaurant and gorgeous staff. Popular with Eurocrats who work nearby, as well as the occasional Belgian politician seeking to lose a few kilos.

417 WORLD CLASS FITNESS CENTRE
Clos du Parnasse 10
Ixelles ⑤
+32 (0)2 503 15 57
www.worldclass.be

This bright, friendly gym draws a lot of its members from the European Parliament. It has several small fitness rooms as well as a good pool. Look out for special deals.

418 ROYAL TENNIS CLUB OF BELGIUM
Rue du Beau Site 26
Ixelles ⑤
+32 (0)2 648 80 35
www.tennisclub-debelgique.be

Here is one of the strangest places in the city. Built in 1954 on top of a seven-story car park, this complex comprises three indoor tennis courts modeled on Wimbledon's. Many of the world's great tennis stars have played here, but it is now a modest club for local players with a tennis workshop and a quaint bar.

419 BAINS DE LA VILLE DE BRUXELLES

Rue du Chevreuil 28
Marolles ③
+32 (0)2 502 53 73

This is a somewhat neglected gem of Fifties architecture in the heart of the Marolles. Swimmers have the choice of two pools, one above the other. The pool on the third floor has big windows at one end which allow you to look down on the roofs of the Marolles. A friendly, curious place.

420 LA PROMENADE VERTE

Bruxelles
Environnement
+32 (0)2 775 75 75
www.bruxellesenvironne-ment.be

A little-known 60km green route for cyclists, joggers and walkers runs around the edge of the city. It includes quiet stretches through parks, wooded valleys and rolling farmland. Easily reached by metro or bus.

419 BAINS DE LA VILLE DE BRUXELLES

The 5 best
SUMMER FESTIVALS

421 BRUSSELS JAZZ MARATHON

www.brusselsjazz-marathon.be
LATE MAY

You don't need to like jazz to enjoy this mellow urban festival held over three days in May. One of the coolest festivals in Europe, it brings together more than 200 performers who play in squares, cultural centres and cafés across the city. Free shuttle buses link the different venues.

422 COULEUR CAFÉ

Tour & Taxis ⑧
www.couleurcafe.be
LATE JUNE

This big urban music festival held at the Tour & Taxis industrial site has a relaxed multicultural atmosphere. Tickets are not too expensive.

423 BROSELLA

Théâtre de Verdure
Parc d'Osseghem ⑧
www.brosella.be
EARLY JULY

You sit under the trees hoping the rain will hold off at this sublime open-air folk and jazz festival. The bands perform in a box hedge theatre hidden in a small park near the Atomium.

424 FEEËRIEËN

Parc de Bruxelles
Central Brussels ①
www.abconcerts.be
LATE AUGUST

Impossible to pronounce, 'Feeërieën' means 'fairy tales' in Dutch. The name neatly captures the essence of this summer music festival, which is held at the bandstand in the Parc de Bruxelles. The street lamps are covered in red cloth and strings of light bulbs hang from the trees to create a magical mood. Concerts are organised by Ancienne Belgique, which ensures some great Belgian bands on the stage.

425 CZECH STREET PARTY

Rue Caroly
Ixelles ⑤
JUNE

In 1997, the Czech delegation hit on the bright idea of promoting their country by hosting an annual street party outside the Czech House in Ixelles. They bring along some wild Czech rock bands, set up a beer tent and a few food stands and – voilà – it's party time.

The 5 best
GUIDED TOURS

---

426 BRUSSELS GUEUZE MUSEUM

Musée Bruxellois de la Gueuze
Rue Gheude 56
Anderlecht ⑦
+32 (0)2 521 49 28
www.cantillon.be

The Cantillon brewery in Anderlecht, not far from Midi station, is the last surviving traditional Gueuze brewery in the city. The cobwebs you see are essential to the brewing process, as is the big open tank in the attic where fermentation takes place. The building is a beautiful 1900 industrial relic, and the owner offers a free glass of Gueuze before you leave.

427 ARAU ART NOUVEAU BUS TOUR

Boulevard Adolphe Max 55
Central Brussels ①
+32 (0)2 219 33 45
www.arau.org

The urban action group Arau has been running tours of Brussels architecture since 1969. The most popular is a three-hour bus tour that looks at art nouveau buildings from the period 1893-1914.

428 PRO VELO

Rue de Londres 15
Ixelles ⑤
+32 (0)2 502 73 55
www.provelo.org

Here is a slow and convivial way to discover the city's secret places. The cycling action group Pro Vélo organises bike tours of the city lasting about three hours. Tours focus on themes like art nouveau architecture, lost cinemas and Magritte.

429 MUSEUMTALKS

www.museumtalks.be

An inspiring initiative in which museum visitors speak about their favourite object in a Brussels collection. The short talks are given in 24 different languages, including Arabic and Chinese.

430 BRUSSELS SIGHT JOGGING

www.brusselssight-jogging.com

A group of passionate joggers organises running tours through the city with occasional pauses to admire the sights. Tours cover central Brussels, the European Quarter and the Atomium district.

426 BRUSSELS GUEUZE MUSEUM

The 5 best places to
PARTY AFTER DARK

—————

431 **K-NAL**

Avenue du Port 1
Central Brussels ⑧
+32 (0)2 374 87 38
www.k-nal.be

It's hard to think of a more cool place than this former warehouse overlooking the canal. It has a vast loft space for dancing and a rooftop terrace that buzzes in the summer. The club hosts the immensely popular Libertine Supersport nights.

432 **MADAME MOUSTACHE**

Quai au Bois-à-Brûler 5
Central Brussels ②
www.madamemoustache.be

This cool, friendly place is decorated in the style of an old fairground, with the DJ based in a gypsy caravan. Expect an eclectic mix of music from 1980s kitsch to Disney hits. The door policy is relaxed and entry is cheap. The cosmopolitan Brussels crowd loves this place.

433 **THE FLAT**

Rue de la Reinette 12
Central Brussels ①
+32 (0)2 502 74 34
www.theflat.be

This original bar hidden in a back street near the Porte de Namur is decorated like a private apartment. You can drink a cocktail in the living room sitting on a sofa, or in the bathroom with your feet in the bathtub, or even in the bedroom lying on the double bed. The drink prices vary during the evening like stock market shares.

434 MR WONG

Rue de la Vierge
Noire 10
Central Brussels ②

Mr Wong has created a sophisticated club in a former restaurant in Brussels' Chinatown district. The art deco interior is warm, deep red and relaxed, while the music is quiet enough to allow conversation. Mr Wong organises parties and gigs from Wednesday to Saturday, though information is hard to track down. Try Mr Wong on Facebook.

435 SPIRITO MARTINI

Rue de Stassart 18
Ixelles ⑤
+32 (0)2 502 30 00
www.spirito-martini.com

This stunning club opened in 2010. It occupies a former 19th century English Church in a dingy back street. The building was transformed by the Antwerp design studio Puresang into a classy venue with three bars and five lounges. Open on Friday and Saturday nights.

The 5 best
SMALL CINEMAS

―――――――

436 CINEMATEK
Rue Baron Horta 9
Central Brussels ①
+32 (0)2 551 19 19
www.cinematek.be

A small door in a side street leads into one of the world's great film museums. The interior was redesigned in 2009 by the Belgian architects Robbrecht & Daem, creating an airy foyer where you can watch fragments from classic movies on suspended screens or tinker with early movie contraptions, but the main reason to come here is to watch a classic film without the background munch of popcorn.

437 VENDÔME
Chaussée de Wavre 18
Ixelles ⑤
+32 (0)2 502 37 00
www.cinema-vendome.be

This art deco cinema on the edge of the Matongé screens serious European and world movies. It now struggles to compete with the shiny multiplexes, but some people still love Vendôme for its tiny pavement box office and its willingness to screen challenging films from Bosnia or Mongolia.

438 NOVA

440 POTEMKINE

440 POTEMKINE

438 NOVA

Rue d'Arenberg 3
Central Brussels ①
+32 (0)2 511 24 77
www.nova-cinema.org

Prepare yourself for a shock. This small alternative cinema run by volunteers looks like a squat. Exposed brick walls, old sofas and car seats are scattered around the bar. But don't run away. This is one of the most exciting arthouse cinemas in Europe, with an ambitious and inspiring programme of experimental films that you will never see anywhere else.

439 STYX

Rue de l'Arbre Bénit 72
Ixelles ⑤
+32 (0)2 512 21 02

It makes no sense. Styx is a tiny two-screen neighbourhood cinema that shows films long past their prime. It should have gone bust years ago, but this adorable relic somehow survives, screening classy European films to audiences that sometimes barely reach double figures.

440 POTEMKINE

Avenue Porte de Hal 2
Saint-Gilles ⑥
+32 (0)2 539 49 44

Frédéric Nicolay has turned an old cinema foyer opposite the Porte de Hal into a hip café with a suspended whale skeleton by street artist Bonom. Classic movies are screened free every evening in an upstairs room that seats just 20. And in summer you can drink a beer at one of the blue metal tables on the square.

The 5 best places to
MEET PEOPLE

---

441 APÉRO URBAINS
www.aperos-urbains.be

Every Friday in the summer months, Apéro Urbains hosts free events in parks or squares. People gather after work to drink and eat, while children run around and DJs play cool music. Invite your friends, pick up a couple of bottles of rosé and you have everything you need for an urban party.

442 FRISKIS & SVETTIS
www.friskis.be

The name is Swedish. It means Healthy & Sweaty. So you know what to expect. The idea is to get fit while having fun. Not expensive.

443 MEETUP
www.meetup.com

A smart concept that started in New York and has now arrived in Brussels. You sign up online and get regular email messages telling you about groups that are meeting in Brussels. They often involve drinks or a meal, but you also get news about culture trips and walks.

444 @SEVEN

Chaussée de Louvain 38
Saint-Josse
www.atseven.eu

Young expats meet up on a Thursday night each month at Mirano Continental to do business, flirt and dance. The venue is an old cinema in a rundown part of town, close enough to the EU quarter to ensure a multinational crowd.

445 PLUX

Place du Luxembourg
Ixelles ⑤

The square in front of the European Parliament is surrounded by bars and restaurants where MEPs, lobbyists and interns head after work. On sunny days, crowds gather on the pavements and in the middle of the square. Best on Thursday evenings, except when the Parliament is meeting in Strasbourg.

The 5 best places for
A CONCERT

---

446 BOTANIQUE
Rue Royale 236
Central Brussels ⑨
+32 (0)2 218 37 32
www.botanique.be

A beautiful venue located in a former greenhouse now lost amid the downtown skyscrapers. The 19th century building is divided into several spaces, from the impressive Orangerie where major bands perform to the cramped Witlof cellar where undiscovered singers perform to a few dozen people. No matter what the music, the Belgian crowd listens attentively.

447 ANCIENNE BELGIQUE
Boulevard Anspach 110
Central Brussels ①
+32 (0)2 548 24 84
www.abconcerts.be

The AB hosts famous singers and bands that sell out a few hours after tickets go on sale, but it also encourages alternative music and new sounds. Bands love the atmosphere and the local bars nearby where they can drink without being mobbed by fans.

448 FLAGEY

Place Sainte-Croix
Ixelles ⑤
+32 (0)2 641 10 10
www.flagey.be

Once listed as one of the world's 100 most endangered buildings, the 1933 Belgian radio broadcasting building on Place Flagey has been converted into a sleek cultural centre hosting concerts, films and debates. The European Film Festival is held here in the summer.

449 BOZAR

Rue Ravenstein 23
Central Brussels ①
+32 (0)2 507 82 00
www.bozar.be

The Palais des Beaux Arts was built by Victor Horta in 1928 as one of the world's first multicultural centres. The current director Paul Dujardin has carefully revived the building to create a vibrant arts venue with a huge programme of classical concerts, exhibitions, film, literary events and kids' days.

450 RECYCLART

Rue des Ursulines 25
Marolles ③
+32 (0)2 502 57 34
www.recyclart.be

A lively alternative art centre located in a disused railway station in the Marolles. During the day, you can drink coffee in the lovely wooden station bar, read the newspapers and watch skateboarders on the square outside. At night, trains rumble overhead while DJs play a mix of rock, house, electro and new wave. Drinks are served at the old ticket hatches.

LEOPOLD II

15 PEOPLE
WHO MADE BRUSSELS

——————

The 5 most famous people
BORN IN BRUSSELS

---

451 HERGÉ
Rue Philippe Baucq 33
Etterbeek ⑤

Georges Rémi, creator of the Tintin comic books, was born in the Brussels suburb of Etterbeek in 1907. Adopting the name Hergé, he began his career by drawing comic strips for the Brussels newspaper Le Soir. The official Tintin museum is in Louvain-la-Neuve, of all places, a 30-minute train journey from Brussels.

452 JACQUES BREL
Avenue du Diamant 138
Schaerbeek

The singer Jacques Brel, famous for songs such as *Ne me Quitte Pas* and *Amsterdam*, was born in Brussels in 1929. He went to school at the Instituut Saint-Louis and began working in the family cardboard factory (the name Vanneste & Brel can still be read on the wall at 18 Rue Verheyden). Brel's career took off in the 1950s after he moved to Paris. His daughter now runs the Jacques Brel Foundation in Brussels.

453 AUDREY HEPBURN

Rue Keyenveld 48
Ixelles ⑤

Audrey Hepburn was born in Brussels in 1929. The daughter of a British banker and a Dutch baroness, she was baptised Edda van Heemstra Hepburn-Ruston. The family moved to the Netherlands when she was ten and she spent the war years in occupied Holland.

454 TOOTS THIELEMANS

Rue Haute 241
Marolles ③

The man with the harmonica who played the haunting theme tune in the film *Midnight Cowboy* was born in 1922 in the working class Marolles district. He was named Jean by his parents, who ran a local café in the Rue Haute. Jean was given an accordion at the age of three, but later took up the harmonica.

455 JULIO CORTAZAR

Avenue Louis
Lepoutre 116
Ixelles ⑥

A statue of Julio Cortázar, the Argentinian writer, stands on the leafy Place Brugmann, opposite the building where he was born on 26 August 1914. His father was in Brussels on business accompanied by his pregnant wife.

The 5 people who
BUILT MODERN BRUSSELS

---

456 **LEOPOLD II**

Brussels was a modest capital until King Leopold II came along with his grand architectural plans. He wanted to make Brussels more like Paris and, thanks to his vast personal empire in the Congo, he had the money to do so. He built the grand central boulevards, the Avenue de Tervuren and the Africa Museum. He also added a Chinese temple, a Japanese pavilion and a wealth of other architectural details.

457 **FRÉDÉRIC NICOLAY**

Frédéric Nicolay has given the city some of its most distinctive bars, such as Mappa Mundi, Belga, Bar du Matin and Potemkine. He also launched the trendy beer Vedett and redesigned an urban square behind Rue Dansaert. Everything he does has a slight nostalgic touch, harking back to an older Belgium.

458 VICTOR HORTA

Victor Horta created some of the most beautiful private houses ever seen in Brussels in a curvaceous art nouveau style. He also designed department stores, the Palais des Beaux Arts and Gare Centrale.

459 PAUL VANDEN BOEYNANTS

Some would say Vanden Boeynants destroyed Brussels. As mayor in the Fifties, he played a major role in organising Expo 58. This led not only to the Atomium, but the creation of a network of urban motorways along former leafy avenues, as well as countless parking garages in the city centre.

460 CHARLES PICQUÉ

As socialist mayor of Saint-Gilles commune and minister-president of Brussels Region, Charles Picqué has been responsible for many of the initiatives that have helped to restore the urban fabric and create a more liveable city.

456 LEOPOLD II

The 5 most
POWERFUL PEOPLE
in Brussels

---

461 **PRESIDENT OF THE EUROPEAN COUNCIL**

The first president of the European Council was appointed in 2009 to give the European Union a leader who could stand alongside the US president. The EU's president is based in the Justus Lipsius building on Rond Point Schuman.

462 **PRESIDENT OF THE EUROPEAN COMMISSION**

The president of the European Commission heads the European Union's bureaucracy. The president's office is on the 13th floor of the Berlaymont Building on Rond Point Schuman.

463 **SECRETARY-GENERAL OF NATO**

The secretary-general of the North Atlantic Treaty Organisation heads the powerful military alliance based in the Brussels suburb of Evere.

464 **PRIME MINISTER OF BELGIUM**

The prime minister of Belgium heads the federal government, which is responsible for areas such as finance and social security. The president is based in the Lambermont residence at Rue de la Loi 16.

465 MINISTER-PRESIDENT OF FLANDERS REGION

The minister-president of Flanders Region heads the government responsible for the Dutch-speaking region of Belgium. As leader of the richest region, the minister-president has considerable political power. The official office is in the Errera House at Rue Royale 14.

PARAKEETS IN BRUSSELS

35 RANDOM FACTS AND URBAN DETAILS

The 5
ODDEST THINGS
about Brussels

---

466 **MADAME PIPI**

Most toilets in bars and cinemas are maintained by a woman affectionately known as Madame Pipi. She is normally found seated at a small table decorated with a vase of plastic flowers, reading a celebrity magazine. She expects to be paid about 50 cents. The tips she receives are her only source of income.

467 **PARAKEETS**

You see them everywhere. And if you don't see them, you hear them. Over the past few decades, Brussels has been invaded by green parakeets. It started in 1974 when the owner of a local zoo released about 50 birds into the wild because, he said, Brussels needed more colour. Now there are an estimated 8,000 colourful birds nesting in the trees on Place Guy d'Arezzo and in several city parks.

468 MUSIC IN THE BRUSSELS METRO

Some years ago, the people who run the Brussels metro decided to stop playing muzak all day. They developed a playlist with songs to match the time of day. The music is cheerful in the morning, becoming more edgy around 4pm when schools come out and ending with classical music after 9pm in a bid to stop kids loitering on the platforms.

469 THE UNDERPANTS MUSEUM

De Dolle Mol
Rue des Eperonniers 52
Central Brussels ①

It once made the list of the ten weirdest museums in the world, but then the Musée du Slip, or Underwear Museum, closed down. The founder, Jan Bucquoy, now displays his collection, ranging from a porn star's panties to a Belgian finance minister's boxers, in the Dolle Mol café. "Underpants worn by Noel Godin on Saturday 18 March 2006 at the Paris Book Fair during the 7th custard pie attack on Bernard-Henri-Levi", reads one label.

470 KING ALBERT'S JACKET

Place des Palais 7
Central Brussels ①
+32 (0)2 545 08 09
www.belvue.be

The BELvue museum has a strange collection of relics relating to the Belgian royal family, but the oddest item is a corduroy jacket in a glass case with a torn sleeve. This was the jacket King Albert I was wearing when he fell in mysterious circumstances while climbing a cliff in the Ardennes.

The 5 best
WORDS IN
BRUSSELS DIALECT

---

471 **SCHIEVEN ARCHITEK**

A schieven architek, or bent architect, is someone who cannot be trusted. The expression dates from the period when a large area of the working class Marolles was torn down to build Joseph Poelaert's monstrous Palais de Justice.

472 **ZINNEKE**

A mongrel dog of the type that Brussels has in excess. It is also the name of a joyful multicultural carnival parade held every two years.

473 **STRONTZAT**

Strontzat means pissed drunk, which is one stage worse than simply zat, drunk, but not quite as bad as strontcrimineelzat, or criminally pissed drunk.

474 **AFKRABSEL VAN METTEKOUWSKLUUTE**

You should use this expression sparingly, as it means, literally, scrapings of a monkey's testicles.

475 **KETJE**

A ketje is a street urchin or, more broadly, someone born and bred in Brussels. Someone recently suggested adopting the term euroketje for someone born and bred in Brussels of EU parents.

The 5 most important days in
BRUSSELS HISTORY

---

476 **25 OCTOBER 1555**

On this day, the Holy Roman emperor Charles V abdicated in the Aula Magna of the 15th century Coudenberg Palace. His son Philip II inherited Spain and the Low Countries, while his other son Ferdinand acquired Germany. The Aula Magna, along with the rest of the palace, was destroyed by fire, but the cellars survive below Place Royale.

477 **13 AUGUST 1695**

On a summer day in 1695, French troops of Louis XIV's army began a bombardment of Brussels that lasted three days. The attack left one third of the city in ruins, including most of the houses on Grand'Place, although the Gothic town hall survived. The ruins were replaced by the Flemish baroque houses still standing today.

478 25 AUGUST 1830

One night in the summer of 1830, protestors stormed out of the Brussels opera house during a performance of *La Muette de Portici*, a romantic opera. They gathered in the street shouting patriotic slogans and took over some government buildings. This marked the beginning of a revolution that led to the creation of the independent state of Belgium.

479 12 OCTOBER 1915

At dawn on this day, the British nurse Edith Cavell was executed by a German firing squad at the national firing range in Schaerbeek. Cavell was working in Brussels when the German army occupied the city in 1914. She chose to stay on and nurse wounded soldiers from both sides of the conflict. But she also helped Allied soldiers to escape from behind enemy lines, leading to her arrest and trial on a charge of treason.

480 25 MARCH 1957

On this day, Belgium and five other European countries signed the Treaty of Rome, which created the European Economic Community. More by accident than deliberate decision, Brussels became the unofficial capital of the organisation.

5 words used in
FRENCH-SPEAKING
BELGIUM, *but not in France*

---

481 SEPTANTE

The French spoken in Belgium is different from the language closely protected by the Académie française in France. The Belgian word for seventy is *septante*, whereas a French person would always say soixante-dix. Ninety is another trap for the unwary. The Belgians say *nonante* while the French fussily insist on quatre-vingt-dix.

482 TIRETTE

The Belgian word for a zip, whereas the French have to employ the cumbersome term *fermeture éclair*.

483 AUBETTE

A newspaper stand in Belgium, but rarely used in France, though it can sometimes refer to a bus shelter.

484 KOT

French-speaking students in Belgium sometimes talk about renting a *kot*. The word is Dutch. It originally meant a hovel or pigsty, but can also refer to a student room.

485 **DRACHE**

Drache is a sudden rainstorm, typical of Belgium. The *drache nationale* is a sudden rainstorm that drenches everyone on the national holiday.

482 **TIRETTE**

The 5 largest
FOREIGN POPULATIONS

486 **FRENCH**

An estimated 46,000 French people live in Brussels out of a total of 190,000 EU citizens. The French blend easily into the city because they speak one of the two official languages. Many settle in the leafy suburbs of Uccle.

487 **MOROCCAN**

At just over 39,000, the Moroccan population is the second largest foreign community. Moroccans have traditionally settled in areas like Schaerbeek and Molenbeek. The Rue de Brabant, near Gare du Nord, and the Rue du Malibran in Ixelles, have strong Moroccan identities.

488 **ITALIAN**

Some 26,600 Italians live in Brussels. Some work in restaurants and snack bars, while others occupy important jobs in the European institutions. They have been settling in Brussels since the 1950s when Belgium looked to Italy to fill its labour shortages.

489 **SPANISH**

Some 19,200 Spanish citizens live in Brussels. The old Spanish community is based around the Gare du Midi, where you find numerous Spanish shops and restaurants.

490 **PORTUGUESE**

The Portuguese community is estimated at just over 16,000, many living in Ixelles around Place Flagey.

The 5 best
BRUSSELS BLOGS

491 **CHARLEMAGNE'S NOTEBOOK**
www.economist.com/blogs/ charlemagne

The Economist's Brussels correspondent posts lucid and always interesting observations on Europe.

492 **BELGIAN WAFFLE**
www.belgianwaffling.com

A homesick London woman with two small children and a difficult dog who blogs about life in Belgium. She posts brilliant observations on the oddest things.

493 **GLORIOUS FOOD AND WINE**
www.onfoodandwine.com

An inspiring foodie blog written by a Eurocrat couple, who have spent the past 15 years eating out and drinking beer in Brussels.

494 **I LOVE BELGIUM**
www.ilovebelgium.be

A beautiful blog with smart observations on Belgian fashion, architecture, photography and design.

495 **BRUSSELS BRONTË BLOG**
www.brusselsBrontë. blogspot.com

A lively literary blog with insights on the Brontë sisters' stay in Brussels.

The 5 largest
INTERNATIONAL ORGANISATIONS

---

496 **EUROPEAN COMMISSION**

The European Commission employs 21.635 people in Brussels. Its main office buildings are the Berlaymont on Rond Point Schuman and the Charlemagne on Rue de la Loi.

497 **EUROPEAN PARLIAMENT**

The European Parliament employs 5.549 people in a complex near Place du Luxembourg in Ixelles commune.

498 **NATO**

The North Atlantic Treaty Organisation has a staff of 4.000 based in a complex in Evere commune, near Brussels Airport.

499 **EUROPEAN COUNCIL**

The European Council employs 3.091 people in the Justus Lipsius building on Rond Point Schuman.

500 **EUROCONTROL**

Eurocontrol employs 2.204 people in a complex at Haren, near Brussels Airport. The organisation coordinates air traffic across Europe.

INDEX

COLOPHON

EDITING *and* COMPOSING – Derek Blyth

GRAPHIC DESIGN – Joke Gossé

PHOTOGRAPHY – Joram Van Holen (www.joramvanholen.be)

D/2012/12.005/3
ISBN 978 94 6058 0925
NUR 506

Third, revised edition, May 2013
© 2012, Luster, Antwerp
www.lusterweb.com
info@lusterweb.com
Printed in Spain by Indice S.L. Arts gràfiques